WILD SONOMA

WILD SONOMA

Exploring Nature in Wine Country

CHARLES HOOD

with Lynn Horowitz and Jeanne Wirka

Illustrations by John Muir Laws

FOREWORD BY JANE GOODALL

Heyday
Berkeley, California

Library of Congress Cataloging-in-Publication Data

Names: Hood, Charles, 1959- author.
Title: Wild Sonoma : exploring nature in wine country / text and
    photographs by Charles Hood with Lynn Horowitz and Jeanne Wirka ;
    illustrations by John Muir Laws ; foreword by Jane Goodall.
Description: Berkeley, California : Heyday, 2022.
Identifiers: LCCN 2022004496 (print) | LCCN 2022004497 (ebook) | ISBN
    9781597145893 (paperback) | ISBN 9781597145909 (epub)
Subjects: LCSH: Natural history--California--Sonoma County. |
    Animals--California--Sonoma County--Identification. |
    Plants--California--Sonoma County--Identification. | Habitat
    conservation--California--Sonoma County. | Wildfires--Environmental
    aspects--California--Sonoma County.
Classification: LCC QH105.C2 H66 2022 (print) | LCC QH105.C2 (ebook) |
    DDC 508.794/18--dc23/eng/20220216
LC record available at https://lccn.loc.gov/2022004496
LC ebook record available at https://lccn.loc.gov/2022004497

Front Cover Art: Shutterstock/jbtphotos
Cover Design: D. Lee
Interior Design/Typesetting: Ashley Ingram and Rebecca LeGates
Maps: David Deis

Published by Heyday
P.O. Box 9145, Berkeley, California 94709
(510) 549-3564
heydaybooks.com

Printed in East Peoria, Illinois, by Versa Press, Inc.

10 9 8 7 6 5 4 3 2 1

Contents

FLOWERS, SHRUBS, AND TREES

INSECTS

The land? We don't manage it, we don't control it—
we are *part* of it.

> —Clint McKay, of the Dry Creek Rancheria
> band of the Pomo and Wappo Indians

———

For Pop, Ramsey, Bella, Riley, Robin, Henry, Teddy, Rex,
Ozzy, Kip, and Watson —L. H.

The well-named song sparrow fills spring mornings with abundant music.

Jane Goodall

FOREWORD

When I was five years old, at the outset of World War II, my mother, sister, and I came to live in my grandmother's house in Bournemouth, in the south of England. The house (from where I write this now) is a five-minute walk from the ocean. From a young age, I spent most of my time in our large and rather wild garden, climbing trees and watching birds, squirrels, and insects. I loved to watch the honey bees push their way into the foxglove flowers and to see how the blooms trembled while the invisible visitor probed for nectar.

Back then, wild cliffs rose up from the beach, and when I was a bit older, I used to spend days with my dog, Rusty, exploring those places—there was no TV and none of the gadgets that are causing so many children today to become disconnected from the natural world. I kept a nature notebook in which I sometimes sketched and painted local wildflowers. I kept caterpillars and watched how they grew, shed their skins, and finally made a chrysalis. Then I witnessed the magic of the butterfly emerging and how its crumpled wings gradually stretched out until finally the transformed insect was ready to fly away.

It is this same love of the details in nature that has inspired *Wild Sonoma*, written by Charles Hood with the help of local naturalist Jeanne Wirka and my good friend the longtime Sonoma County resident Lynn Horowitz. The starting point for saving our planet from its destruction is for people to share an appreciation for the wonders of the local natural world around them. Once you get to love the natural world, you want to protect it.

I have been to the Bay Area many times over the years, including Sonoma, so I know firsthand about the special beauty of this county. The recent terrible series of wildfires has wrought much devastation to the natural landscape, altering the stability of local ecosystems.

But one of my reasons for hope has always been the resilience of nature. Sure enough, after the first little sprinklings of rain, small brave green shoots pushed their way up from the blackened, fire-scorched land. Such is the resilience of nature. Seeds, lying dormant in the ground, sprang to life, and baby trees appeared. Those little seeds were waiting, ready to renew life, to bring hope after the horror of the fires.

Wild Sonoma: Exploring Nature in Wine Country is a book for our times. It provides an introduction to the natural and unnatural forces shaping our environment, then offers an informed and lively field guide to common plants, animals, birds, and insects one is likely to encounter on a hike in Sonoma. Lastly, it suggests a set of special excursions to experience Sonoma's varied natural landscapes.

The last time I was in Sonoma, I spent the night in the Horowitzes' tree house. I awoke to the joyful melody of song sparrows singing "hip

hip hooray all, spring is here!" reminding me of how much there is still left to celebrate in the plant and animal kingdoms. Let us hope that we can save the wonders of our natural world for generations to come. Let us each do our part before it is too late.

Welcome to Wild Sonoma!

INTRODUCTION

Wild Sonoma celebrates the diversity and importance of the natural world, and wants to help us all better appreciate—and better access—our natural heritage. Not only is nature all around us, but we want to share our idea that experiencing nature does not need to feel like hard work. You do not need to get up super-early to see nature, nor keep a log of how many sweaty, buggy miles you hiked. In fact, you don't even have to hike at all. Some places in this book are great for kayaking, some for mountain biking, some for riding horses, and some can even be enjoyed right from the parking lot. Got kids and strollers? No problem—many of the sites listed here are perfect for the little ones too.

Part 1 opens with a look at what makes "here" *here*. If the Russian River watershed produces some of the best wine in California—forgive our bias if we say that it does—how

1

The greater Sonoma area offers hundreds of miles of trails.

did those mosaics of *terroir* come to be? In this section, we think about the fundamentals of any ecosystem: water, soil, air, fire. By focusing on Sonoma County, we are able to go in-depth to look at the connected dance between habitat and nature, and also to provide new ways of thinking about wildfire.

Part 2 is a field guide introducing iconic and commonly encountered species. Illustrated by the always astounding John Muir Laws, the field guide surveys sixty-two plants and animals you may have seen before but may not know much about, and also will introduce new things that will be exciting to encounter once you know to watch for them. This section could be ten times longer, of course—the bird list alone could have included another two hundred species. We tried to focus on plants and birds and insects everybody can easily see and, in fact, probably already *has* seen, and just didn't have the right name for yet. From ants to redwoods and from hawks to butterflies, we hope you will find lots here to linger over and enjoy.

The book ends with six excursions that take you deeper into wild Sonoma, from the popular, well-known Spring Lake Regional Park to the longer, wilder hikes of Sugarloaf Ridge State Park. Sugarloaf has bears, mountain lions, remote trails, and even an observatory for nighttime exploration. The hikes allow us to suggest some places to go, but each sample trip also will add more information about the species and ideas presented earlier in the book.

A central idea is that Native American perspectives on nature and landscape exist in the present tense. Sonoma's Pomo, Wappo, and Miwok Indians preceded the Russian, Spanish, and Anglo-European settlers by thousands of years, and their cultures and perspectives remain vital today. Trip 2, a walk along the Half-a-Canoe Trail at Lake Sonoma, provides an

The underwings of the pipevine swallowtail sport brilliant orange spots.

A coot's lobed foot opens and closes like an umbrella. See page 33 for the full "Darwinian" story.

opportunity for us to share what we have learned from Clint McKay, a member of the Dry Creek Rancheria Band of the Pomo and Wappo Indians, whose deep knowledge of plants and landscape stewardship is truly inspiring.

Together, these six featured sites will give you a delightful introduction to the riches all around us. Surprised (or angry) that we didn't include your favorite place? Look for the appendix (Where to Go Next) that follows the last section; we close with an overview of additional regional sites.

Nature can mean many things to many people. For us, the term always includes words like *joy, wonder, discovery,* and *celebration.* We hope this book embodies all those terms. Thank you for joining us on this amazing journey.

Skippy says, "A hike is always more fun when you bring your dog."

Part 1

WHERE NATURE COMES FROM

Boaters enjoy the Russian River at Guerneville.

As pieces of the planet go, Sonoma brings home all the first-place ribbons. There are forests and meadows, swift rapids and calm backwaters, wild seascapes and delicate flowers. The animals too are diverse. There are black bears and mule deer, bobcats and beavers. Acorn woodpeckers "yak" tree to tree, and even on Highway 101, you can spot the stately grace of a passing heron or see sentinel oaks crisply outlining the crest of a ridge in the morning sun. Within an hour of leaving the Bay Area, you can access hundreds of trails, trails that will allow you to see lizards and newts, ferns and redwoods, grasslands and foggy mountaintops. How much nature is there? Here's one number worth noting: ornithologists comparing notes have come up with a county-wide sighting list of over 450 bird species.

To understand how Sonoma came to be as interesting and varied as it is today, it helps to look at the processes that unify all habitats.

Every ecosystem starts with the same ingredients: sunlight, air, water, and soil. As we look around us, we may see only a very bright daytime star, a blue sky, some rocks, and a covering of green plants. But what we can't see is that the plants in the sunlight are converting water and carbon dioxide into sugars and oxygen, which in turn nourish the birds and animals—including all of us—that rely on plants for food as well as for the air we breathe.

And as we look more closely, more attentively, we can see a million years laid out at once. Every hill and creek is the result of geology dancing with rainfall, and that geology is a nonstop parade of churning, grinding, lifting, and folding. There are cobbles in the drabbest, scrubbiest backyard that first started out as a diaphanous cloud of silt slowly settling on the floor of a warm, shallow sea many millions of years ago. Other layers of sediment pressed down on top of that—at first resting as lightly as a duvet on top of a feather mattress. And then over time, magic happened: silt became mud, mud became sandstone, and sandstone got subducted under a rising tectonic plate, heated, melted, and made anew. Nature is the ultimate recycler: a clot of mud washed into an ancient sea ends up as cut and dressed stone turned into walls to terrace the soil that grows our grapes. The rock we skip across a pond today will sink to the bottom, but it won't be there forever. Some future morning, it will be on the top of a mountain or buried deep under a tectonic plate, on its way to melting back into magma and reemerging somewhere else. We walk on the roof of time with each and every step.

WATER AND WATERSHEDS

This is the Golden State, but it also is the water state, and California always has at least *some* rainfall, even in drought years. Most years we might want more of it, but there is always water arriving and departing, sitting still or rushing away. Some water sneaks in unnoticed, coalescing as beds of dew and fog. Some winters, we can see snow frosting the highest Sonoma ridges. The snow may melt after a week or even an hour, but that snow contributes to the cycle of water.

Each trickle and rivulet makes its way into (and over) the soil and shows up downstream later using the slow-motion delivery systems of springs and creeks and sag ponds and meadows. Unlike other parts of California, in Sonoma, our wells and reservoirs rely only on local sources, not a distant Sierra snowpack.

The term *watershed* refers to a specific radius of landscape that collects, stores, and delivers water to an end point—usually a river (such as the Russian) or an ocean (the Pacific). At the high points of a given watershed—the summits and main ridges—the rain that falls on one side may drain to a completely different outlet than the rain that falls a foot to the right, which will flow into a different system.

You can see the Russian River watershed outlined on the map on page 12. The Russian River starts east of Willits, then follows 101 south— more accurately, one might say that the 101 followed it, not the other way around—through Redwood Valley to Ukiah. The main channel continues south past Cloverdale, Geyserville, and Healdsburg, bending west at Windsor to wave hello to Guerneville on its way to the sea at Jenner. In dry years, the upper and middle parts dwindle to a flow so meager, children can safely wade and splash midstream. Yet in winter it can turn roads into lakes, and closer to Jenner, the Russian River can become a surge of raging brown water.

During a winter flood, the Russian River overtops its banks near Healdsburg.

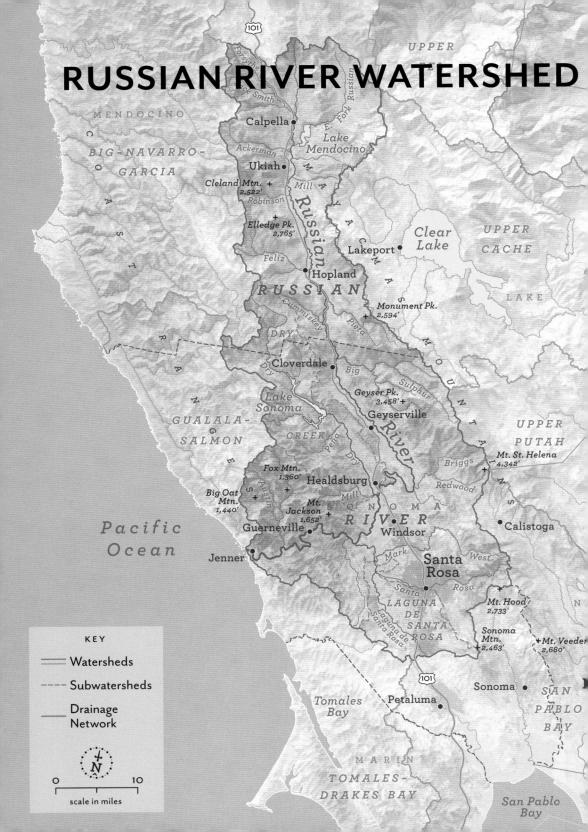

RUSSIAN RIVER WATERSHED

UPPER

MENDOCINO

BIG-NAVARRO-
GARCIA

Calpella

E. Fork Russian

Lake
Mendocino

Ukiah

Cleland Mtn. +
2,522'

Robinson

Elledge Pk.
2,765'

Feliz

Hopland

Lakeport

Clear
Lake

UPPER
CACHE

LAKE

RUSSIAN

Monument Pk.
2,594'

Cummiskey

DRY

Piera

Cloverdale

Big

Sulphur

Geyser Pk.
3,458' +

Geyserville

Lake
Sonoma

CREEK

DRY

River

Fox Mtn.
1,360'

Healdsburg

Peña

UPPER
PUTAH

Briggs

Mt. St. Helena
4,342' +

Redwood

Big Oat
Mtn.
1,440'

Austin

Mt.
Jackson
1,652' +

Mill

S O N O M A

Guerneville

Pacific
Ocean

Jenner

Mark

R I V E R

Windsor

Calistoga

West

Santa
Rosa

Rosa

Santa

LAGUNA
DE
SANTA
ROSA

Mt. Hood
2,733' +

Sonoma
Mtn.
2,463' +

+ Mt. Veeder
2,680'

101

Tomales
Bay

Petaluma

Sonoma

SAN
PABLO
BAY

MARIN
TOMALES-
DRAKES BAY

San Pablo
Bay

KEY

Watersheds

Subwatersheds

Drainage
Network

N

0   10

scale in miles

Following the idea of watershed, all the rain that falls inside the marked area on the map ends up in the river itself or else soaks into the aquifer, which is long-term underground parking for water. Some of the water there may be thousands of years old—tap into it cautiously, because once it runs out, the aquifer may need another thousand years to fill back up again. And just to be clear, an aquifer is not an underground lake—you could not drill a tunnel and arrive at a big cave, ready to host subterranean jet ski races—instead, an aquifer represents soil that is so saturated that water fills all the pores between the particles. When groundwater reaches the surface (following a fault line upward, for example), it creates artesian springs. When it passes by lava or other geothermal activity along the way, then it becomes hot springs, like the Old Faithful Geyser in Calistoga.

For its entire 114 miles, the Russian River still represents nature every inch of the way. When it overflows into the Laguna de Santa Rosa, it supports the most biologically rich region in the entire county and the largest freshwater wetland in all of northern California. This is also a stopover for thousands of migrating birds on the Pacific Flyway every year. Yet because the river has undergone so many interventions, the river is a case of "nature plus us." Two dams (Coyote, 1958, and Warm Springs, 1982) created Lake Mendocino and Lake Sonoma (159), storing the winter runoff that keeps the river alive in summer. Some lakes, like the ones in Riverfront Regional Park (173), are former gravel pits that have been allowed to fill back up and become places where humans, otters, and osprey all can fish.

Among those fish are the really "big 'uns," the salmon. They may be thirty inches long and weigh ten pounds, and a really monster specimen can top thirty pounds. In California, four species of salmon can occur: Chinook, coho, pink, and chum. (The last two are mostly strays from farther north.) All salmon and their near relative, the steelhead trout, are anadromous, meaning that they are born in fresh water and return to home rivers to spawn, while spending the rest of their lives at sea. Changes occur as they return to fresh water, so that Chinook salmon go from blue to red and develop a hooked beak like a parrot. This is a one-way journey; the fish will die at the end of it, and their bodies and nutrients will rejoin the larger cycle of death and rebirth.

To help maintain salmon populations today, water is released from dams in summer to allow access to spawning areas, while hatcheries release small fish ("fry") to increase the base stock. Water from the bottom of dams is cooler than water in sun-cooked shallows, which is also important for spawning. Strangely, even fire helps: megafires create so much smoke for so long that sometimes the smoke's shade cools the water.

Overall, the news is mostly good. Despite the dams and diversions, despite the decline of Chinook or the presence of rambunctious crowds on holiday weekends, the Russian River and its 238 tributaries still offer much to celebrate. The watershed encompasses fifteen hundred square miles, and inside that area you can find sixty-three species of fish, plus

LEFT: Coho salmon spend their lives at sea and return to fresh water to spawn.
RIGHT: Look for blue dashers along the edges of still ponds.

an uncountable bounty of otters and foxes, newts and frogs, tanagers and jays. We are delighted to share that bounty with you.

DIRT VERSUS SOIL

What we call "dirt" in casual, everyday English is something much grander than that. From an ecological perspective, there is very little "dirt" here, because we don't have dirt; we have something better: soil. The difference is that dirt is dead and soil is alive. Alive with what? Alive with everything: worms, bugs, fungi, bacteria. And rich in other ways, too—speckled with bits of eggshell or the head of a rusty nail or slivers of petrified wood or even the humble seeds from tarweed and dandelions. Soil is a garden of life and potential life. That life may wait a long time (for a drought to end or a road to peel away in a landslide), but life, on average, is deeply patient. You cannot make a garden grow out of just dirt, but you can raise vegetables in soil, and when you come in from gardening and wash your hands, your hands are not dirty, they are soil-y.

Soil formation typically takes thousands or even millions of years, as rocks erode into clay and silt and sand, and as organic matter decays and accumulates (or washes downstream to accumulate someplace else). Yet if we speed up the time-lapse camera, it is quite a wild bronco ride. "Tectonic uplift, faulting, and down-warping valleys are all going on before our very eyes," says geologist Terry Wright. "Downslope movements, sheetwash, flooding, uplifting river terraces, rapid erosion, and transportation of materials all happen continuously, and further complicate soil formation and distribution."

Aboveground roots hint at the complexity of the many connected processes under the surface.

Vintners like to say there are more varieties of soil in Sonoma than in all of France. The wine regions of Sonoma (shown on the map on page 20) owe their varietal plentitude to the many microsoils provided by weather, fate, and the number of times in the past the earth has split open and roared with bright-red fire. Mount Saint Helena can be seen from many vantage points in Sonoma and Napa; it is two million years old and just tall enough to catch a bit of snow most winters. This peak is an extinct volcano, and volcanoes have been active in Sonoma from one hundred million years ago to as recently as ten thousand years ago. Much of that heat is still present; it drives Sonoma's hydroelectric energy sources and churns the hot springs, mud baths, and steam rooms of the region's storied spa industry.

Iron and other minerals from volcanoes help create varied soil profiles, which in turn contribute to the *terroir* of a given vineyard. This French word has become a bag of infinite holding, since each wine lover seems to interpret it slightly differently. It has to do with the ineffable sum of parts, including soil, drainage, weather, the degree of slope of the land the grapes have been planted on, what time of day the clouds usually cast shadows, how sweetly the bluebirds sing, what color bandana the scarecrow wears, and many other criteria besides. *Terroir* resembles the Spanish word *duende* (spirit, passion, authenticity)—it is hard to explain, but you will know it when you taste it.

Besides the organic material stored in it, and besides all the bending and kneading done by erosion and faulting, soil has a third magical property.

Underneath the surface, out of view of all of us "abovegrounders," plant roots talk to other plant roots through an elaborate network of tiny fungal threads called mycorrhizae. This word connects two ideas—*myco* means "mushroom" and *rhizal* means "root." Some call this network

Dirt or soil? (Answer: *soil.*)

Witches' butter and turkey tail fungi work together to break down an old log.

"nature's internet." It turns out that soil is buzzing with shopping lists and marriage proposals, temporary alliances and long-term loans. Scientists are slowly starting to figure out the roles mycorrhizal fungi play in keeping a given piece of forest healthy. One thing the experts agree on is that mycorrhizal fungi can be found in almost all plant systems, and another is that everything interconnects. According to Lorenzo Washington, these fungi "take up important nutrients from the soil, passing them to plants in exchange for sugars and fats."

This is all microscopic; even the most robust fungal tendrils are barely visible to the human eye. So tiny are these fungal threads, a single cubic inch of soil would contain eight miles of filaments if they were laid end to end. It is not just small—it is also ancient. Lorenzo Washington again: "Fossil evidence of [mycorrhizal relationships] dates back 400 million years, and it is quite possible plants and their fungal partners existed before plants with [traditional] roots." The news being traded might be an alert about an invasion of pest insects, or the availability of a patch of sunlight after an old, canopy-dense tree has blown down in a winter storm. If we could insert a microphone under the surface, the soil would pulse and flare with the roar of a thousand conversations at once.

Aboveground, our choices can help or hinder this underground network. In Sonoma, organic farmers, many winegrowers, and conservation ranchers now list soil health topmost on their agendas. Good soil health is important for sequestering carbon, storing water, and making the land resilient against the damage of droughts, floods, and fires. In vineyards, for example, winegrowers plant cover crops between the rows of grapes to increase the soil structure and its capacity to hold nutrients.

What may seem like just dirt is as important as sun, rain, and the entire web of life.

WINEMAKING REGIONS

MENDOCINO

Lakeport

Hopland

101

175

Clearlak

LAKE

PINE MTN./
CLOVERDALE PEAK

Gualala

Sea
Ranch

Black Pt.

LAKE SONOMA
WILDLIFE AREA
ROCKPILE

Lake
Sonoma

Cloverdale

Middletown

Warm
Springs
Dam

ALEXANDER
VALLEY

29

Geyserville

SALT POINT
STATE PARK

Horseshoe Pt.

DRY CREEK
VALLEY

Salt Pt.

FORT ROSS/
SEAVIEW

AUSTIN CREEK
STATE REC. AREA

Healdsburg
NORTHERN
SONOMA

KNIGHTS
VALLEY

128

ROBERT LOUIS
STEVENSON
STATE PARK

Calistoga

FORT ROSS
STATE HISTORIC PARK

SONOMA
COAST

River

Windsor

CHALK
HILL

S   O   N   O   M   A

NA

116

Russian

RUSSIAN
RIVER
VALLEY

FOUNTAINGROVE

101

29

He

GREEN
VALLEY

12

SONOMA COAST
STATE PARK

Sebastopol

Santa
Rosa

TRIONE-
ANNADEL
STATE PARK

BENNETT
VALLEY

Glen
Ellen

Bodega
Bay

MOON
MTN.

Bodega
Head

Pacific
Ocean

Bodega
Bay

Rohnert
Park

SONOMA
MTN.

12

SONOMA
VALLEY

Sono

POINT REYES
NATIONAL
SEASHORE

Tomales
Bay

Petaluma

116

LOS
CARNERO

121

MARIN

Novato

37

KEY

Vineyards

**SONOMA
COAST** Vitcultural Areas

State and Federal
Parklands

N

Point
Reyes

Lighthouse

Drakes
Bay

SAN PABLO BAY
NATIONAL
WILDLIFE REFUGE

San Pable
Bay

GOLDEN GATE
NATIONAL
RECREATION AREA

101

San Rafael

0   10

scale in miles

The History of Winemaking in California

Native grapes in the American West are edible, but do not produce good wine. For communion service, the Franciscan padres needed better options. Wine in California thus starts with the missions. The initial Mission grape stock came from Spain by way of Mexico, and as with horses, longhorn cattle, adobe bricks, and cochineal dye, wine grapes carry with them a lingering taint of colonial legacy. We see that even in the name, since the original grape is still called the "Mission grape."

Even after the mission system ended, the plants lived on—and could be dug up from the abandoned missions and transplanted elsewhere. By the 1830s, relocated Mission grapes were being grown commercially in and around the pueblo of Los Angeles, watered by ditches from the Los Angeles River and harvested by recently displaced Native Americans. The first French vines were imported into California at the same time.

The gold rush created twin demands for table grapes and wine, and the Los Angeles–San Francisco trade flourished. But why import if you can grow crops locally? By the 1850s, the first Northern California wineries were established, using a mix of Mission and European root stock.

Within thirty years, a very successful industry had developed, investigating such questions as which wood made the best barrels—American oak or French oak, French oak or redwood?

Prohibition hit California wineries hard. It was still legal to drink alcohol—bars and restaurants and grocery stores just could not sell it. People turned to bootleggers and bathtub gin, and then in 1929, to make it way worse, there was the Great Depression. When the laws were finally repealed in 1933, 95 percent of the old growers were out of business.

It was difficult to come back. Culturally, there was a myth that all French wine was good and all American wine was rubbish, so it was hard for wineries to market their products.

That changed in 1976. Almost everybody has heard of the blind taste test—held in France, using French judges—in which California wines kicked French butt. A reporter from *Time* magazine helped turn the upset into international news. Adios, amigos: there is a new kid in town, and his name is Chardonnay, his name is Malbec, his name is "Thank you, server, yes I do believe I will have another glass." The 1976 win was not a one-off. In multiple competitions since then, the quality of Sonoma wine has been verified again and again.

Grape growers face a difficult future, and the varieties grown in fifty years may not be the same ones as those harvested now. (Is there a way to graft wine grapes onto prickly pear cactus?) There are water questions to answer and such topics as the fair treatment of the laborers, and the best ways to regenerate soil for future harvests, future generations. The history of wine in California is one of challenge and invention, and the story is still evolving.

Residents evacuate from the
Glass Fire, Calistoga, 2020.

FIRE AND FIRE ECOLOGY

Two things are equally true: California was meant to burn—it's how
nature works here—but it was never supposed to burn this hot or this
often. People who study wildland fires use the term *fire return interval*,
which basically means the average pause historically between one
typical fire and another. Hundreds of years ago, when Native American
stewardship still controlled the burn patterns, you might have many
very small fires in a mosaic across the landscape. There may have been
just as many fires per year as we have now, but as fires go, they were
brief, cool, and local. Most trees could recover and the fuel load was
controlled, which in turn meant that large, contiguous, unstoppable
fires were rare.

In recent years, the North Bay Area as a whole has seen large fires
nearly every year. (See the map on page 26.) In Sugarloaf Ridge State
Park, the 2020 Glass Fire (67,484 acres; 1,555 structures destroyed) came

on the heels of the 2017 Sonoma Complex Fire that ultimately burned more than 250,000 acres and destroyed eighty-nine hundred structures. Between the two fires, 99 percent of the park burned, and of that area, half of it burned twice—a fire interval of three years. Fire historian Stephen Pyne says that we don't live in the Anthropocene but in the *Pyrocene*. As he remarks, "We often speak of an epidemic spreading like wildfire, but it makes equal sense to speak of a fire spreading like a plague, a contagion of combustion."

This is our own doing. We have so many big, hot fires now because we had too many years of misguided fire suppression. Bad science, misguided timber management practices, and rising global temperatures have combined in terrible ways. We now know that trying to keep fires from happening at all just makes them worse when they do come. And then there are the external factors, such as drought and heat domes and rising temperatures. Beetle infestations weaken trees, and invasive grasses ignite easily. There are more roads now, which in turn means more dry grass right beside cars, and those cars emit sparks (or even catch on fire themselves). And of course, miles and miles and miles of high-voltage power lines crisscross the landscape. According to one report, Pacific Gas and Electric was responsible for fifteen hundred California fires in just six years, including the Camp Fire in 2018.

Let us pivot away from the bad news. And we do want to acknowledge that the bad news is seriously and irrevocably sad. In the Sonoma Complex Fires and the Glass Fire and so many others, people died, historic wineries burned, thousands of families lost their homes. At the same time, we should remember that wild Sonoma has had other terrible fire years, such as 1964 (Hanley Fire; 53,000 acres); in 1923, the Guerneville Fire burned from Armstrong Woods downslope to Guerneville and west all the way to Jenner. Large, serious, life-altering

LEFT: Aerial relief: the S-64 Sky Crane can deliver 2,650 gallons of water and retardant.
RIGHT: In California, this needle seems always to be stuck on the right edge of the dial.

fires have occurred, past tense, and will continue to occur, future tense. We cannot change that, but one thing we can do is change how we think about fire.

It is not correct to say (as news reports often do) that such-and-such fire "destroyed" *x* quantity of forest. Altered it, perhaps, but not *destroyed*—the original land is still there, under the red Phos-Chek retardant and the gray and black ash, which means that afterward the plants will be back as well. The species mix may be different, but the plants and the animals and the all-important fungi will be back, and with them the rest of the living world. No California fire is ever so hot or so total that nothing will grow afterward. Nature endures. We don't even need to tell it what to do. "Nature has more pathways than humans have tools," Stephen Pyne reminds us, "and more information coded into genomes and biomes than people have ideas."

One reason for hope is that even in the largest, hottest fires, there is often a mosaic afterward—inside the fire's footprint, some places are less fully burned than others, and in some instances, the fire is driven by such a strong wind that it hurricanes through a stand of trees without igniting them all. This mosaic pattern helps regrowth and diversity. It provides refuges for the remaining wildlife and a seed bank that can help adjacent areas regrow. One term to impress your friends with is *pyrophilous fungi,* which refers to the mushrooms that only come out after a fire. Another common expression is *fire following,* referring to those plants that come up after a burn.

Gray pine is an example of a plant that tolerates (and even needs) fire. Mature trees have thick-enough bark to withstand an average fire; the cones actually require fire to melt the resin that normally seals them shut. Seeds grow better if scarred by heat and if the ground itself is cleared of competition. This species is an important part of the oak-pine woodland; the cones produce copious seeds that were (and are) eaten by Native Americans and that are also enjoyed by squirrels, jays,

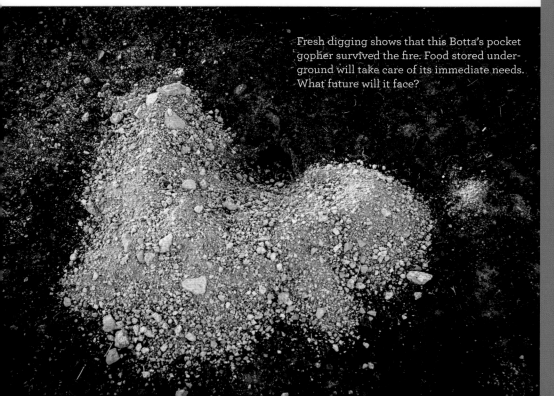

Fresh digging shows that this Botta's pocket gopher survived the fire. Food stored underground will take care of its immediate needs. What future will it face?

RECENT FIRES

Ukiah

Lakeport

Hopland

Clearlake

M E N D O C I N O

Clear Lake

L A K E

Gualala Pt.

Cloverdale

Valley
76,084 acres
9/12-10/6
2015

Middletown

Lake Sonoma

Horseshoe Pt.

Salt Pt.

Healdsburg

S O N O M A

Kincade →
77,762 acres
10/23-11/10
2019

Glass
67,484 acr
9/27-10/2
2020

St. Helena

Lake Hennes

Tubbs
36,701 acres
10/8-11/1
2017

Santa Rosa

N A P A

Nuns
55,798 acres
10/8-10/31
2017

Pacific Ocean

Bodega Bay

Rohnert Park

Sonoma

Na

Petaluma

Sears Point

Tomales Bay

Novato

San Pablo Bay

Vall

Point Reyes

M A R I N

Drakes Bay

KEY

Historic Fire Perimeters

Fire Notable Recent Fires Names

Developed Areas

N

0   10
scale in miles

Bolinas Bay

San Rafael

C O N T R C O S T A

Richmond

San Francisco Bay

Golden Gate

Berkeley

San Francisco

and deer. According to Clint McKay (interviewed on pages 160–167), you can even use gray pine resin as chewing gum.

Many small plants are fire followers, such as Brewer's calandrinia, a tiny herb with gorgeous magenta flowers. According to the California Native Plant Society, it "spends most of its life cycle as a tiny seed in the soil seed bank, waiting for fire to coax it aboveground to flower, fruit, and set seed—before the seeds return again to their secret life underground. Amazingly, they can live dormant in the seed bank for 80 years or more."

Of course as with all aspects of our complex planet, the role of fire is complicated, and an overly hot fire can sterilize soil. Yet a typical fire of typical intensity can make a flush of nitrogen available for successional plants. Phosphorus and calcium are also recycled into the soil after a fire. Depending on the next season's rainfall, ash-fertilized soil produces exceptional wildflower blooms the following spring. Lupines, for example, often recolonize burned areas quickly, as does ceanothus brush. If your property has been visited by fire, the silver lining can be a lush display the following spring, including many flowers you have never seen before.

What happens to the fire-following plants as fires increase in frequency and intensity? Nobody is quite sure, but that may be where you come in. Community science can help in a dozen ways—for example, by documenting the succession of plants through apps such as iNaturalist and Calflora or by joining a bio-blitz like the Rare Plant Treasure Hunts hosted by the California Native Plant Society. You may be the person who finds the best and rarest plant of all.

Finally, a word of pragmatic advice from us authors, all of whom have been affected by fires over the past few years. Please make sure you have a go-bag, an evacuation plan, and the courage to use them both.

Part 2

A FIELD GUIDE TO COOL AND INTERESTING LOCAL SPECIES

ACORN WOODPECKER
Melanerpes formicivorus

This is a bold, noisy woodpecker dressed in black, white, and red. It is found in oaks and urban forests.

* Clown-faced with vivid head pattern
* Rolling flight; white "silver dollars" on each wing
* Found near oaks but also on telephone poles, houses, even palm trees
* *Yakkity yakkity* calls (loud and social)

TREES FULL OF HOLES, HOLES FULL OF ACORNS

Vivacious and easily seen, acorn woodpeckers live in family groups and harvest acorns. They drill storage holes, then pound in acorns—one per hole, hammered tight. One tree can have up to fifty thousand holes. Typical site is a dead oak, but it could be a sycamore, phone pole, fence, barn, or house. If the acorn dries and shrinks, it gets shifted to a smaller hole. A tight nut is a good nut—jays and squirrels can't pry it out.

Acorns are collected in fall and eaten in winter. In summer, acorn woodpeckers flycatch and take ants, termites, and beetles in midair. They also glean directly from the trunk. A final trick is to drill holes in a tree until sap oozes out, creating a "trap line." Each day, the bird visits to eat the sap, plus any insects caught in the amber goo.

ALL TOGETHER NOW

The basic social unit is ten to sixteen related birds. They forage for food and defend trees communally. They also practice cooperative nesting. This means they carve a hole (or enlarge an existing one); it might be in the granary tree or one nearby, and one group of woodpeckers might create multiple nest holes. More than one female will contribute eggs, and the group raises the hatchlings communally. This "sister-wife" approach ensures that each bird has some genes that get passed on. Acorn woodpeckers can also leave their home troop and join new bands up to ten miles away.

Ecologists call the acorn woodpecker a keystone species, since so many things depend on the work it does. Nest and roost holes are later used by screech owls, house wrens, tree swallows (64), western bluebirds (68), and Vaux's swifts. Western gray squirrels (132), an important player in the "let's keep forests healthy by having good fungi" game, use acorn woodpecker holes as den sites.

 A woodpecker's tongue wraps around its skull, under the skin. This helps cushion the skull while the bird is hammering away.

AMERICAN COOT
Fulica americana

A round-bodied black "duck" of lakes and ponds, the coot bobs its head as it swims. If it is walking on the shore, notice the green, lobed feet.

* Often in flocks near water (parks, lakes, golf courses)
* Black; white beak can show a dusky tip and a red knob on forehead
* Croaks and grunts and squawks (*priiiik*)—never goes "quack"
* Juveniles gray, the chicks rusty brown

COMING TO A PARK NEAR YOU

The coot just can't get no respect. It's part of the rail family (as in, "thin as a rail"), a group of slender marsh birds that slip through the reeds. Coots do like marshes, but they swim like ducks and congregate in the open. They don't fly well, and as they swim, the head jerks back and forth. Even the name sounds bad, thanks to expressions like "crazy as a coot" or a "bunch of coots and codgers, sitting on the porch."

Linguistic prejudice aside, this vegetarian pond dweller proves that you don't have to be flashy or elegant or a gifted songster to survive. You won't find it in the forest or the ocean, but few bays and lakes don't have their own coot flock.

DARWIN IN ACTION

The coot's foot has to solve several problems at once. On marshy ground, you want to spread your weight out—you want to be wearing snowshoes, not high heels. But to walk among reeds, you want a slender foot that folds out of the way between steps. And then when swimming, you want broad surfaces, like a snorkeler wearing swim fins. Coot feet have lobed toes that can spread wide or fold up like a closed umbrella, depending on what shape is most needed.

One look-alike species is the common gallinule, formerly called a moorhen. The gallinule is a similar shape and color, but a bit smaller and more likely to be tucked out of sight in the reeds, and has a red, not white, beak.

Many birds' taste buds are not on their tongues but along the insides of their bills. The coot can "taste" a new plant by nibbling with its bill tip.

AMERICAN ROBIN
Turdus migratorius

The "robin redbreast" is a plump, rusty-tummied bird of lawn and garden. It might perch on a fencepost or sing from the middle of a leafy tree.

- Midsize songbird; both sexes dark gray with a cinnamon-red belly

- Hunts on the ground or pours out a liquid song from post or tree

- White crescents above and below eye; streaked white throat

EVERYBODY'S FAVORITE BACKYARD BIRD

Lovely to look at, lovely to hear ("cheerio, cheerily"), the American robin checks all the boxes for why people love birdwatching. In northern parts of North America, the arrival of the robin often means the end of winter and the start of spring. No wonder it is a perennial favorite on bird calendars.

This bird is a thrush, so it is neither huge nor dinky and often is seen on the ground or the lower half of the tree. Other thrushes in our area include the varied thrush, which has blue and orange breast stripes, and two brown kinds: the hermit thrush and the Swainson's thrush, both of which have tan backs with white bellies and black spots. All of these have a profile similar to a robin and act like it too, even if they look very different. This is a good case for learning the "gestalt" of a group and then being able to recognize others from the same clan.

GENERALISTS, UNITE!

Robins are not picky. They will nest in parks, on a farm, and around houses, but also in forest or even the open prairie. And they eat from both sides of the menu: fruit and berries when they can, or worms and beetles, or snails, or caterpillars and grasshoppers. Robins can investigate the undersides of leaves (like a warbler), sit quietly on a branch and then sally out (like a flycatcher), or patrol a well-watered lawn, ready to tug an earthworm out of the soil (because "the early bird gets the worm"). They will come to backyard feeders, but if you want to be a robin's best friend, try offering mealworms. Unlike juncos and sparrows, robins do not eat birdseed.

 Homesick Puritans thought this New World species looked like Europe's robin, which is also red. They gave it the same name, even though the original robin is a small flycatcher, not a plump thrush.

MALE

FEMALE

ANNA'S HUMMINGBIRD
Calypte anna

Small but feisty, the male Anna's hummingbird has a magenta throat and a pugnacious attitude.

* Long beak and too-fast-to-be-seen wingbeats
* Magenta throat and head (males); a few magenta throat spots (females and young males)
* Both sexes: green back, gray belly

FAST HEART, FASTER WINGS

The smallest bird in the world is a hummingbird (in Cuba). In another "did ya know," the typical hummingbird's heart beats twelve hundred times a minute. They can flap their wings seventy times a second. The tongue is so long, it coils inside the skull like a party favor, and at the very tip, almost too small to be seen, the tongue forks in two, increasing the surface area when lapping up nectar. The Anna's weighs about an eighth of an ounce, and the nest is willow down or lichen flakes woven together with strands of spiderweb.

There are no hummingbirds in Africa; the world total of 325 species is only found in the New World, and they are mostly concentrated in the tropics. Counting stray, once-every-hundred-years species, California has fourteen species of hummingbirds on the official state bird list.

EATING YOUR WEIGHT IN SUGAR

Humans and hummingbirds are equally addicted to sugar, and depending on the species, hummingbirds consume from 0.5 to 8 times their body weight in nectar every day. Unlike humans, hummingbirds know when to leave the sugar alone and start hawking for midges. They also follow sapsuckers to filch sap from holes in willows and oaks. Flower nectar by itself does not provide adequate protein, and especially when a female is getting ready to lay eggs, she supplements her diet with flies, gnats, and spiders. To get minerals, Anna's also will eat ashes or strips of paint. In trade for all the free nectar, the flowers that hummingbirds visit want them to get faces smooshy with pollen. This happens often, but the hummingbirds do not eat pollen directly.

Anna's is a hummingbird of the American West, with records from Alaska to Baja. It is our expected hummingbird; most spend the winter here. (In winter, hummingbirds can get nectar from nonnative species such as blue gum eucalyptus.) Many native plants attract hummingbirds, so we encourage planting flowers such as California fuchsia—they brighten the garden, and the hummingbirds they attract will brighten the soul.

MALE

FEMALE

CALIFORNIA QUAIL
Callipepla californica

Heard more often than seen (*chi-CAHH-go*), this plump mini-chicken of grassland and oak woodland is often in groups of ten or even fifty.

* Round body, short legs; only flies short distances (often downhill)
* Black-and-white face, checkered belly, white accents flicked along each side of the body, and a perky top feather
* Females plainer, with a smaller top feather
* Feeds on ground, but sentinels watch from posts or low branches

ULTIMATE SURVIVOR

This is a legal game bird in California, so there is a substantial harvest each year, yet quail still remain visible and common. They eat mostly seeds and buds, scratching under the brush and walking single file through grass, but also will take beetles, spiders, ants, and snails. They eat berries too, including poison oak. Small, hard seeds can be tricky to digest; chicks may acquire the necessary gut fauna by pecking at adult feces.

LOCAL YET INTERNATIONAL

When British birdwatchers speak about working their local patch, they mean a nearby marsh or park they visit regularly, all the seasons of the year. For this quail, its local patch is local indeed: the radius of a quail's life span may fit inside a ten-mile circle. Nests are in dense grass or tucked up under a forgotten tree; these birds can lay up to sixteen eggs twice a year, helping keep the population balanced against all the creatures that want to eat them, from bobcats to peregrine falcons. In the hottest parts of summer, California quail do need water, though not a lot of it, and if it's a bit brackish or downright salty, they can make do. In winter they may not drink at all, since wetter, more lush vegetation during the rainy season lets them meet their needs that way.

The feather on top of the head is sometimes compared to punctuation. Some books call it a question mark, other books an apostrophe. California quail have short, powerful legs, and when threatened, they prefer to run rather than fly. A line of baby quail running after their mother, with the characteristic forward lean, can be a very charming sight.

Found from British Columbia to Baja, the California quail shows up in backyards or the edges of parks, but mostly is a bird of brushland, native grasslands, and oak woodlands—which is to say that, in Sonoma, it can appear just about anywhere.

CALIFORNIA SCRUB-JAY
Aphelocoma californica

This is a blue and gray and noisy and curious backyard and forest bird. It has no peaked crest, so is not the other local jay (Steller's).

- Solo or in flocks, with a gray saddle across an azure back
- *Shreeenk shreeenk* call (plus twenty more squawky, scolding noises)
- White eyebrow on a blue face; pale throat; gray belly
- Never any crest on the head

WHEN IS A BLUE JAY NOT BLUE?

All blue jays are blue, except when they are not. In Texas there is a green blue jay and an all-brown one, and Northern California has the Canada jay, which is gray with a dark cap. Our two expected jays here are the

California scrub-jay and the Steller's jay, which is all-blue above and below with a black head and jaunty mohawk.

Jays are larger than sparrows and bluebirds, but smaller than magpies and crows. All jays are corvids, meaning they are noisy, social, deeply clever animals. Of our two, Steller's jays most often stay in the woods (including nonnative species), while scrub-jays are more often seen in neighborhoods and oak woodlands. Scrub-jays focus on acorns, especially in winter, but like all corvids they are generalists, and scrub-jays will hunt lizards, investigate roadkill, raid a cherry tree, or try to cadge a sandwich crust at your picnic.

WORK SMARTER, NOT HARDER

We can say of a difficult person that he is a tough nut to crack, but for scrub-jays, ain't no such thing. An acorn, for example, is a very hard shelled seed. A scrub-jay can hold it still with a dexterous foot, hammer down with precise strikes of the bill, then pry open the crack to get out the meat. They also open walnuts that way. Like the oxpeckers of Africa, scrub-jays know how to find ticks on the bodies of mammals—in this case deer, not zebras—working the body end to end.

A single scrub-jay can cache five thousand acorns in one season, putting each one in its own hole or crevice and memorizing the location. Jays will forage in loose flocks, but when it comes to caching, each bird goes its own way. In fact, if one jay suspects another jay has been watching it, it will move the treasure to a better place later, once the snoops have left.

COMMON RAVEN
Corvus corax

Note the hefty beak, the whooshing wingspan, and the voracious curiosity. Crows are slimmer, smaller, tamer. Crows caw while ravens croak and gargle and go *kok kok kok*.

* All black, including head (turkey vultures have red heads)

* Wedge-shaped tail (on crows, squared-off tails)

* Fierce, powerful bill (crow's bill is slimmer, more jay-like)

* Can do aerial acrobatics (crows don't soar or tumble)

DUMPSTER DIVAS AND YODELING YODAS

Ravens use tools, solve problems, and remember their enemies. Hands down, they are the smartest animal in this book. Compared to us, they spend less time per day going to work and more time playing and napping and messing around. Bath time in a deep puddle or even park sprinklers can be a communal festival of preening, scratching, stretching, and head tossing. They *grok* and croak with immense variety; according to one source, ravens have "a repertoire of at least 20 distinct calls of known function, 79 call types distinguished spectrographically, and many mimicked sounds, and numerous utterances of unknown meaning."

Among other things, they share information about good places to find roadkill, which humans are kind enough to supply freely. In presettlement times, they would have had to follow wolves to forage at kills, but now our highways are the killing fields. Other food items include trash, snakes, lizards, mice, eggs from any bird smaller or less attentive than it, insects, fruit, grain, and even commercial pistachios, which they knock off of the branches, de-hull, and eat on the ground under the trees, leaving the shells as evidence of their raiding.

NOT CROWS

Crows are related to ravens, but are a separate species. Ravens have shaggier throats, beaks that are more hooked, a more "fingered" look to the wings, and more of a diamond- or wedge-shaped tail. You are more likely to see a crow messing about in an orchard or hanging out in a town park than you would a raven. Instead, look for a raven on top of a mountain, perched on a dead snag, surveying its demesne. (Out of our area, ravens do well even in the Mojave Desert, where they are a serious problem for baby tortoises.)

If you've seen any of those TV programs wondering what nature will look like after humans go away, it's a good bet that there will be at least three animals left postapocalypse: the coyote, the cockroach, and the common raven.

DARK-EYED JUNCO
Junco hyemalis

The junco is a tidy songbird with a pink bill and black head. It often forages on the lawn or path with towhees and other sparrows.

* Small (sparrow size) and often in mixed flocks
* Pale bill stands out against a dark head
* Long tail edged in white (very noticeable in flight)
* Forages in the open: lawns and open understory

ONE MODEL, MANY PAINT JOBS

The same species of junco has half a dozen color patterns, with names for the subforms including "slate-colored" or "pink-sided" (which is tan, not pink). Most of the juncos you will see are called "Oregon" junco. The male has a black hood, brown back, and gray belly. The female is similar but more gray headed. On both sexes, the pale bill stands out cleanly, and on all the juncos, if they are startled, their white-edged tails show vividly.

Juncos are seedeaters, or mostly so, though they won't say no to a random spider or a low bush overburdened with berries. If you have a feeder, they will tidy up the mess left on the ground by other birds. Among many potential threats, Cooper's hawks want to eat them, which means that foraging time out in the open always must strike a balance between gathering food and ensuring safety. The white tail flash disorients a cat or hawk about to take a swipe.

HEY GUYS, WAIT UP!

When not singing to attract a mate or defend territory, feeding juncos keep in touch with flock mates using short, high chip notes, in a loose sort of "I'm here, are you here?" checking in. Its song is a long melodious and steady trill. If disturbed, a flock may twitter in a rush of notes as everybody flies up to the safety of a nearby tree. If a bad guy shows up— an owl or snake or loose dog—then the juncos join other ground birds in mobbing the intruder. The combined flock circles around the danger, scolding and pishing.

Juncos breed here and are resident year-round, though we also host out-of-town winter visitors. Nationwide, juncos move back and forth like an immense, six-month-long tidal surge. Summer sees the wave of juncos wash up against the top edge of Alaska and Canada, and then in winter the wave rolls back south, filling up the bottom of the Lower 48 and northern Mexico.

BREEDING ADULT

JUVENILE

DOUBLE-CRESTED CORMORANT
Phalacrocorax auritus

This long-necked waterbird feeds by chasing fish underwater. Afterward, it spends the rest of the day on rocks or snags, drying its wings in a "spread-arm" posture in the sun.

* Duck size and long necked; mostly dark

* Fresh water, salt water, or lagoons

* Yellow or orange base of bill

* Wings are held in the sun to dry

THREE BIRDS IN ONE

When swimming, the cormorant's body is often low in the water, while the neck and head form an upside-down L. In flight, cormorants often form a loose V like migrating geese, but often with their necks showing a bit of kink or bend, creating a skinny Z. Perched on shore, they can be upright and compacted, with the neck sometimes hardly visible at all, or else wide armed like a martyr on the cross, drying their short, broad wings in the sun.

Adult feather color is matte black or dark brown; immatures are blotchy tan. On adults, the base of the bill can be orange, especially in summer. Breeding adults also have turquoise-green eyes and blue eyelids—pass the mascara.

IF IT AIN'T BROKE . . .

Cormorants eat fish, plus eels and the odd frog or vole. Dinner ranges from minnow size to a foot long. The chase is swift and sure, and small fish will be swallowed underwater. Larger or spikier food items, such as a crayfish or sculpin, need to be brought to the surface and dealt with by shaking or thrashing. A flick of the head and down the gullet it goes.

The reason cormorants spend time drying off in the sun is due to oil, or rather, the lack of oil. Their feathers are not as densely coated with oil as those of other waterbirds, which makes them less waterproof. The sleeker, wetter feathers provide less drag underwater. In all, cormorants are an example of a successful, durable design. Their body plan and hunting methods may be direct and unrefined, but as a group, they are found worldwide, and their basic structure has been stable for millions of years

 Cormorants can see well underwater, but also catch fish just by feel if it's after dark.

WHITE-CROWNED SPARROW

GOLDEN-CROWNED SPARROW

GOLDEN-CROWNED SPARROW
Zonotrichia atricapilla

This boldly marked sparrow is here from October to May. A sister species has a white-and-black (not yellow-and-black) crown; both can be seen foraging with juncos (44).

- Black-and-yellow blaze on top of the head
- Usually feeds on the ground or low in bushes
- Woodlands, grasslands, parks, and backyards
- Easily recognizable sad song

A SPARROW WORTH NOTICING

If we spend a moment with sparrows, we will see that they can be as brightly marked and as interesting as other birds—it's not their fault they're not as large as an eagle or as loud as a peacock. The golden-crowned is a large sparrow and easy to see, with that lovely yellow blaze down the center of the head. Fabulous!

A sister species, the white-crowned sparrow, winters in yards and brushlands. Adults of that kind have cleanly marked white-against-black stripes on their faces and heads. Juvenile white-crowned sparrows have tan stripes and can be harder to identify compared to the brighter adults. The great thing about birdwatching is that if you see something that doesn't quite fit, that's fine. Just say "Who cares?" and move on. You can always try again tomorrow.

"NIMBY" BIRDS

Both golden-crowned and white-crowned sparrows are vegetarians. Like the junco, they eat seeds, buds, small fruits or berries, young plants, and—if anybody is offering—birdseed at feeders, and they don't mind sifting through the leftovers underneath a feeding station as well. The stray spider or two ends up in that buffet, as do termites, ants, and other insects, but plants and seeds make up a majority of the winter diet.

Calls include *chinks* and *peenks* and other chip notes. The main song, delightfully emo, is a minor-key set of descending notes best described as "oh dear me." (Another version is "I'm so weary.") We have an idea that birds are happy when they sing and that their songs express joy. If we could put most bird songs into English, they actually would be some version of "Hey, suckers, clear off—this is my thicket!"

GREAT BLUE HERON
Ardea herodias

America's largest heron is slate blue with a six-foot wingspan.

* Gray body with black stripe on white face

* Solitary in grassy fields, lakes and rivers, coastal lagoons

* Calm, stately flight, with neck folded and legs straight out behind

* Active both day and night

NOT A CRANE

Great blue herons walk slowly through the water, looking for frogs, fish, and crawdads, or else they pick a good spot (right above a gopher hole, for example) and wait—and wait, and wait. Even if it takes hours, when the chance comes, *pow*, down goes the spear-tipped beak and the snake-fast neck, and just like that, quick as lightning they've grabbed another meal.

They can be seen along rivers and lakes, in ditches and ponds, or in open fields.

A lot of people call these birds cranes, but the sandhill crane only rarely shows up in greater Sonoma. Flocks of them winter nearby, however, in the rice fields near Sacramento and Davis. Like a great blue heron, the sandhill crane is also tall, gray, and heron-like, but it often occurs in small groups, and it never flies with the neck folded.

BACK FROM THE BRINK

Places like the Everglades have even more kinds of herons than California does, and those other species stray to California every once in a while. Sometimes it's fun to look at a bird book just to see all the "what if" birds, such as the reddish egret or the yellow-crowned night-heron, species that could turn up one time out of a million but are easier to spot in a marsh in Texas or Florida. One thing that the Sunbelt herons share with our birds is a "back from the brink" history. That is because this bird and the next species (great egret, 52) were hunted for plumes for ladies' hats in the nineteenth century. The National Audubon Society got its start in reaction to this senseless harvest. Egret and heron populations have recovered now, and for the most part the population numbers are stable.

Herons and egrets are colonial nesters (see the Ninth Street Rookery spotlight, page 181), which makes them vulnerable to disturbance, since so many are in one loud, noisy, communal space. Luckily our traditions have evolved, and most people leave the birds and their nests alone. These days, we would all rather see them than wear them.

GREAT EGRET
Ardea alba

This large white egret is nearly as tall as a great blue heron, but is all white with black legs, black feet, and a yellow bill. It can be found in wetlands, along rivers and lakes, or in open fields.

- Tall—similar in size to the great blue heron
- All white with a yellow beak (snowy egret has a black beak)
- Black legs and black (never yellow) feet
- Usually solitary; can be by water or in a grassy field

STICK WITH THE PLAN, STAN

The great egret is great in several ways: size, beauty, and especially success, since it is native to many, many countries around the world. In North America, it is a summer resident in much of the Lower 48 (and sometimes Canada), with year-round status in California, coastal Texas, and Florida. But it also is found in all of Mexico and Central America, the Caribbean, much of South America, much of Africa, in India and Southeast Asia, and across most of Australia. Strays have even reached the sub-Antarctic islands south of New Zealand. This worldwide range shows that once you get a template that works (body size, adaptability to different food sources, efficient flight that easily reaches 25 mph), don't mess with success.

Great egrets are arguably the most beautiful and statuesque birds of our wetlands, and they become even more striking during breeding season. Their faces turn a bright green, and long feathers called aigrettes grow from their backs. These lovely plumes almost drove this species to extinction because they were hunted for women's hats.

LOOK-ALIKES AND KISSING COUSINS

The snowy egret looks like the great egret, but is smaller and has black legs. But the bill is dark, not light, and the snowy egret has vivid yellow feet (which it uses to attract and/or startle small fish). The cattle egret is more common in the tropics than in Sonoma, though there are some records. It too is white and is the size of a snowy egret, but it is stockier and has yellow legs, a yellow bill, and, sometimes, yellow head plumes. It likes fields and cattle; in Africa it follows cape buffalo. A bird that breeds in the same rookeries as great egrets is the black-crowned night heron. White bellied, gray backed, and dark capped, it too is a small, stocky heron, limited to rivers and ponds (never fields), and it often hunts at night. Last, the green heron is slate green and chestnut, with yellow legs. It is small and discreet, tucked under leaves at water's edge, unseen but ready.

MALE

FEMALE

HOUSE FINCH
Haemorhous mexicanus

Come for the male's red colors and stay for the gorgeous song. Common feeder and yard bird.

* Streaky brown finch with a rinse of bright red on head and chest
* Females and young males plainer (some can show yellow)
* Backyards and woodlands; attracted to feeders

BEAKS, BILLS, AND SEED BASHERS

It may seem counterintuitive, but to identify tricky "brown job" birds, forget about color (which can change depending on time of day, angle of view, or what the bird has been eating) and look instead at the structure, especially the bill shape. In small birds, most are either crushers or stabbers.

Birds that eat seeds (finches and sparrows and buntings, for example) have short, stout, nutcracker bills. Insect-eating birds such as warblers and wrens have slim bills that can jab and pry. The house finch is an archetypal seedeater: that short, stout, triangular beak is great for cracking nuts and seedpods, while the fine tip is surprisingly adroit. Houses finches come readily to bird feeders, but warblers almost never do.

Males are redheaded, but the red's intensity varies, depending on what the bird has been eating. The brighter the color, the better the diet and hence the healthier and more ecologically successful that individual can claim to be. Females and younger males are streaky brown.

RED VERSUS PURPLE, AND HOUSES VERSUS PINE TREES

Sonoma has a house finch look-alike, the purple finch. They are the same size and color plan, but the purple finch shows more raspberry-colored red (the house finch is more orange), and the purple finch has softer, blurrier streaks. Female purple finches have a more dark-and-light face pattern, with an obvious pale eye-stripe setting off a dark cheek. Purple finches come to feeders too, but are more likely to be seen in denser woods, less often in fields and towns. Their songs help distinguish them. The house finch song is busy, jumbled, and gossipy sounding ("Did you hear what happened in school today?"), and ends with a sharp buzz. The purple finch song, by contrast, is smoother and more melodic.

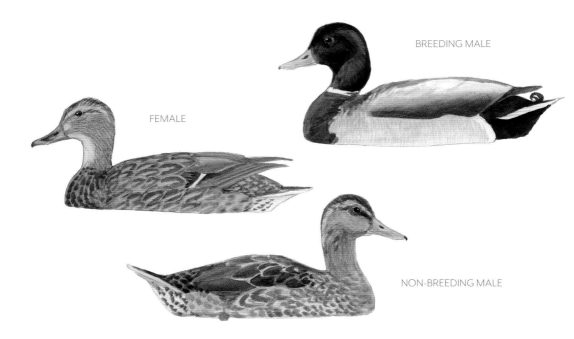

FEMALE

BREEDING MALE

NON-BREEDING MALE

MALLARD
Anas platyrhynchos

This green-headed, orange-footed, yellow-billed quack-quack duck is well known to all.

* Males distinct, but molt to all brown during the "eclipse" phase
* Females always streaky brown, with a blue-and-white wing patch
* May feed on lawns or fields, but return to water eventually

HOW TO BE WIDESPREAD AND COMMON

Three words describe mallards: *omnivorous, opportunistic generalists.* That means the list of what a mallard eats includes snails, larvae, acorns, leftover grain in harvested fields, shrimp, frogs, crayfish, pond weed, sedges, nestling birds, berries, and pieces of bread tossed out by well-meaning (but nutritionally ignorant) park-goers.

They are equally casual about habitat, generally sticking to rivers and lakes, but in their native range (from the Aleutians to Mexico), they seem never to have met a ditch, marsh, field, or slough they could not call home.

You may have seen a hawk or raven with a gap in wing feathers, since they molt in sequence, one feather at a time. Ducks molt all at once, going into eclipse plumage at summer's end. The male is temporarily all brown, and for about a month, ducks can't fly. Their wing feathers have not grown back in.

THEY DO PAIR UP (BUT DON'T MATE FOR LIFE)

Wild mallards pair up on wintering grounds or early in spring, and select a nest site together. That can be a scrape in a marshy, protected area, or even a floating mat of vegetation. The nest is made from grass and stems within easy reach and then layers of down feathers the female plucks from her own body. Mallards do not mate for life; once the young are born, the gentleman goes off to muck about with other males. If the nest fails, in the wild usually that is it for that season, though park ducks may raise multiple broods.

Park ducks also grow tame easily and may become strident if you show up at pond's edge and are not ready to feed them their allotted tribute. Park ducks come in many color combos. The ones with knobby red faces are Muscovy ducks, but most other park ducks started out as mallards.

 Only females go "quack." (Males just give a strangled little rasp.)

MOURNING DOVE
Zenaida macroura

This slim dove is pinky-tan, long tailed, and widespread. The soft *whoo-cooo-oo* call sounds sad, even forlorn—hence the name. Taking off in a sudden, launching flight, mourning doves also emit a squeaky whinny, which is made by the wings and may startle predators and alert flock mates.

* Slim and delicate (unlike the chubby, head-bobbing park pigeons)

* Small, round head; no black hind-collar (unlike the similar Eurasian collared dove)

* Long, tapered tail and small black spots on the wing

* Can be seen on the ground, on phone wires, or in trees

THE "GOOD NEWS" BIRD

The mourning dove may be the most plentiful native bird in all of North America. The call may sound mournful, but the facts are not: one estimate counts 350 million mourning doves overall, and that is despite the 20 million a year that get shot by hunters.

The shape and color combine to make the mourning dove easy to identify, or nearly so. A nonnative species, the Eurasian collared-dove, has a similar buff color. That one is a larger bird overall, with a lot of white in the tail and a distinct half-collar of black marking the back of the neck. Mourning doves, even if silhouetted on a power line at dawn, will always look smaller headed and longer tailed.

Rock doves (also called rock pigeons) are the city pigeons that you see on buildings and in vacant lots in urban areas. They are bigger still, piebald or gray, and often have a dark head and a little white mark on top of the bill. By size alone, pigeons are as easy to tell from a mourning dove as a bowling ball is from a badminton birdie.

BILLING AND COOING

Nests are typically up in a tree on the edge of a wood near grasslands, but can be built on the ground or in a rain gutter of a house or in the middle of a cholla cactus or even on top of an unclaimed nest previously made by a robin or jay. Both sexes help incubate eggs, keep nestlings warm, and feed young. Pigeons and doves produce a kind of "milk" from the linings of their throat, which is used for a few days, and then regular food is regurgitated after that. (Some penguins do this too.)

The mourning dove is a widespread generalist of open country—towns, yards, fields—but rare inside dense forest. The population is remarkably stable, which is something to "crow about" in an era of bad news.

IMMATURE

ADULT

RED-TAILED HAWK
Buteo jamaicensis

Broad chested and wide winged, this hawk circles slowly on afternoon thermals, revealing a fan-shaped, rust-red tail.

* From below, chestnut tail and dark band of hash marks across chest

* In flight, broad, wide wings with visible "fingers"

* Open country including coast (not inside forest)

IT HAS A RED TAIL (EXCEPT WHEN IT DOESN'T)

The usual features—chestnut tail, dark breast band, and often a dark edge on the forefront of the wing—help identify most in-flight red-tailed hawks. Yet some can be all dark, or so pale they're nearly white, and juveniles have no red in the tail until the second year. The basic ratio of wing to tail to chest won't change, though, and most versions have a breast band and red tail (even if not as legible as usual).

The red-tailed hawk eats rabbits and everything else that size, from snakes to rats to gray foxes. Its hoarse, screaming *kee-eeee-arr* call carries a long way and is familiar to almost everybody, since if you have not heard it hiking, you've heard it on television. Producers use it as a generic soundtrack cue for bald eagles, ospreys, kestrels, and space aliens.

EYES LIKE A HAWK

All raptors have stereoscopic vision, and if you were a hawk, you could spot a gray mouse on a gray sidewalk from the top of a ten-story building.

Hawks have two eyesight powers we don't. One is the ability to see into the ultraviolet range, which may help them detect urine trails from rodents. The other is target acquisition. A hawk has to keep a running ground squirrel in focus while diving at 120 miles an hour. Imagine you are in a batting cage, facing a series of knuckleballs being shot straight you. How many could you track at once? Yet a hawk does this each time it hunts. One word: *wow*.

Female raptors are larger than males, which may make them better incubators; or, because both attend young, different body sizes may offer access to a wider range of prey.

MALE

FEMALE

RED-WINGED BLACKBIRD
Agelaius phoeniceus

This blackbird is a noisy and colonial inhabitant of reedbeds. Males flash red shoulder patches.

* Larger than sparrow or finch (almost robin size)
* Males all black with scarlet-over-yellow shoulder patches
* Females dark streaky brown; both sexes have a stout, conical bill
* Loud *CONK-uh-ree* song from reeds in lakes, ponds, and ditches

BRAGGADOCIO IN THE BULRUSHES

Bold, loud males assert dominance by calling from a perch above a marsh or reedy lake and flaring their shoulder patches. The *CONK-uh-ree* call is loud and emphatic, though when foraging, both sexes keep in touch with a simple but decisive *chek*.

Red-winged blackbirds eat insects in summer, seedheads and grain in winter, and in winter especially, they can move out into fields or roadsides to forage in large, swirling, mixed-species flocks. Look for these birds by lakes, ditches, ponds—any place with intact reeds and adjacent fields for foraging. Over time, the yellow borders on a male's shoulder patches can wear down and be hard to see, but if you have an all-black blackbird with no red anywhere, then it could be another kind, described next.

BREWER'S BLACKBIRD (BONUS SPECIES!)

Another blackbird seen locally is all black, but the male has bright, sewn-on pale-yellow eyes, sort of like an animated sock puppet. Native to meadows in the Sierra, Brewer's blackbirds accept parking lots and grassy lawns as close enough. Seen in good light, males are purple and green (never true for red-winged) and females are an even, dark brown, not streaky like a female red-shouldered blackbird.

The great-tailed grackle is all black, and it too whistles and squawks, but it is bigger than either a Brewer's or red-winged blackbird, and the male grackle has a glued-on-sideways tail shaped like a canoe paddle. Female grackles are similar to males, but tan-brown (never streaky).

 Males hunch their shoulders and flash their red markings to defend their territories. The more red a male has, the more attractive he is to females.

TREE SWALLOW
Tachycineta bicolor

Tree swallows arrive in spring and are small, fast, and pretty as they swoop and bank to hawk insects over rivers and ponds.

* Blue-green above with white below, but no white rump patch
* Rests on snags and power lines, but in flight always fast, acrobatic
* Often over (or near) water

THE GOOD KIND OF CAVITIES

What do swallows swallow? Water, for one thing—they drink on the wing—but mostly flying insects: dragonflies, caddisflies, mayflies, stoneflies, bees, ants, moths, spiders, beetles, and grasshoppers. In winter, if insects are hard to come by, swallows can survive on fruit such as bayberries, and before breeding they sometimes eat bits of eggshell

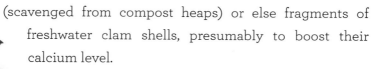

(scavenged from compost heaps) or else fragments of freshwater clam shells, presumably to boost their calcium level.

This species is present year-round, though more abundant (or at least more often reported to eBird) in spring and early summer. Tree swallows are cavity nesters, looking for old woodpecker holes or just rotted parts of a tree branch. That is a problem, since looking for those same holes are bluebirds, flycatchers, chickadees, starlings, wrens, and other tree swallows. Nest boxes help, but mostly we need more woodpeckers and more dead trees. A tidy landscape is, in the end, an empty landscape.

LIKE BUT NOT ALIKE

Other regional swallows include barn swallows (dark blue above, cinnamon below, long tail wires); cliff swallows, which make mud nests, such as under the edges of overpasses on I-5; and the violet-green swallow, decked out in similar colors but with a white rump. Young tree swallows are brown and look like northern rough-winged swallows, but those are a paler, dingier brown above and have a brown-gray wash on their head, chest, and throat. Purple martins are dark blue (not purple) and are the ones that you see cute houses built for, looking like a colonial mansion but with twenty chambers, stuck up high on a pole on the edge of a field.

Swifts are even swifter, with thin, arcing wings and cigar-shaped bodies. Several species are possible here, though none are common. If it is gray, that makes it a Vaux's swift (the *x* in the name is pronounced); if there is black and white, it's a white-throated swift. There are a few Sonoma records for black swift, which nests on cliffs behind waterfalls.

TURKEY VULTURE
Cathartes aura

Vultures soar on thermals, expending minimal energy as they search for carcasses using smell. At night they roost in trees or cliffs, often communally. When the day warms up, off they go.

- Hawk size and all-dark, with a naked red head and white beak tip
- Soaring flight with wings held in a V, often teetering from side to side
- Year-round here; other populations migrate to Central and South America

BALD IS BEAUTIFUL

Durable and tough is the business plan. Dark feathers contain melanin, which helps fortify against wear, and a bald noggin means feathers won't get food on them as the vulture sticks its head inside a dead deer's tummy. We can envy their immune systems, since they can eat spoiled meat that even a feral hog can't handle. No worry about salmonella or botulism (or anthrax or cholera). Their guts can process almost anything, and if an animal has died from disease, they sanitize the site by removing tainted meat quickly.

Historically vultures could rely on condors for help in opening up large, tough hides. Now that they are on their own, they have to wait on time to soften up the meal, or they enter through the animal's nose or anus. Once in, they can be adroit in their autopsies, stripping tendon from bone, or, with a skunk, eating everything except the scent glands.

HALT OR I'LL VOMIT ON YOU

Jockeying with other vultures at a carcass, they will feint and hiss. Dominance is more fluid than linear—Who's bigger? Who got there first? Who is so hangry they will take on all comers?

Vultures mate for life—*we think*. They are understudied, as are most ugly animals. And while vultures lack the vocal structure to sing, they do have their own private range of noises, and during mating they will emit "harsh, rapid hissing-grunts." Afterward there will be eggs and a nest, which will need to be defended. Vulture parents guard their nests vigorously. Don't get too close, or *blat*, they can projectile vomit out to a range of ten feet. Given what they eat, this must be a toxic brew indeed.

MALE

FEMALE

WESTERN BLUEBIRD
Sialia mexicana

Bluebirds chase down insects from a low branch; small flocks mob berries in winter. One of our most attractive residents.

* Male is blue above, rust red below; often flycatches over open ground
* Female is plainer, though can show orange wash
* Year-round resident

MISTLETOE—IT'S NOT JUST FOR KISSING UNDER

Bluebirds are flycatchers in summer and berry pickers in winter. Summer insects are chased down from a fence post or low branch, so bluebirds like edge habitat: meadows or fields, but with perches and forest or brush nearby. If the cooler months still have an abundance of insects, then the birds will continue to take those, but if not, they switch to elderberries, poison oak, mistletoe, and wild grapes—any kind of fruit or berry that will get them through winter.

Spring means breeding, and because bluebirds are cavity nesters, they have the same housing shortage as tree swallows (64). Both male and female halves of the pair help search for nest holes and defend them once they find one. If your yard or park has the right habitat, consider putting up bluebird nest boxes.

IS NATURE MORE LIKE *BAMBI* OR MORE LIKE *THE SOPRANOS*?

Just as we know that mourning doves are not really in mourning, we also know that songbirds do not sing because they are happy or because they want to greet the dawn or because they find the arrival of spring especially joyful. The male bluebird has a lot going on. He has to patrol his territory and kick out interlopers, keep a lookout for foxes and gopher snakes and Cooper's hawks, find enough grubs and flies to feed himself and his family, keep house wrens from trying to bogart his nest hole, and, all in all, be the biggest, baddest hombre on the block.

One study from 1996 reports that while chasing rivals, "males may grab opponents' legs, causing both combatants to fall to ground." Once there, the "aggressor may pin opponent on his back by standing on him, spreading wings wide over opponent; from this position, aggressor may strike vigorously with its bill." Studies show that despite rigorous enforcement, up to half the eggs have out-of-territory fathers.

ARROYO WILLOW
Salix lasiolepis

If this streamside tree or tall shrub is present, that means water is nearby. It often grows in thick stands. This is a pioneer plant after floods. Deciduous: loses some or all of its leaves in winter.

* Large shrub or small tree
* Long, tapered leaves
* Streams and wet areas
* Releases copious pollen "dander" in spring

RIVER'S SHADE AND BIRDS' OASIS

Willows are water lovers. They also grow thickly, and willow stands attract wildlife, from the common yellowthroat to mourning cloak butterflies, which use it as a host plant. Bushtits and other flocking birds can be found there too. As one birder jokes, "Take a picture of a willow in migration and there usually is a warbler somewhere in the photo."

Habitat and leaf structure are two clues for identification, as is size—this species rarely grows taller than thirty feet, and dense, ten-foot-high walls of willow are common along the edges of the Russian River.

The bark contains the raw ingredient for the first forms of aspirin, and ethnographic studies of almost all California tribes mention different ways willow bark was utilized, from being seeped as tea or chewed directly. Active coppicing—trimming stumps so they produce slender rods—creates the flexible struts needed for basketry.

BAY LAUREL
Umbellularia californica

The bay is a leafy, medium- to large-size tree with fragrant leaves that you can use for cooking.

* Found in many habitats, from river bottoms to mountaintops
* Long dark-green leaves that are sharply fragrant
* Small green to purple fruits that look like tiny avocados
* Other names: California bay, pepperwood, Oregon myrtle

VARIABLE VARIABILITY

The bay laurel can be a six-foot shrub or a sixty-foot tree. It likes floodplains and river bottoms, but also follows ravines up onto the hillsides and can even be found in open chaparral. Bays can tolerate serpentine soils (193) and stay green year-round. The leaves are long like those of willows, but are more spaced apart on the branch. The strong scent comes from chemicals the tree produces to ward off insects, deer, and other would-be herbivores.

The other common name, pepperwood, refers to the seasoning-like smell of the crushed leaves. It is related to the kind of bay from the Old World that people cook with, and you can indeed liven up a stew with fresh or dried California bay, but be sparing until you find the quantity that works best (and use caution: some people are allergic). There is

a Pepperwood Preserve (200), but this plant is found many places, not just there. (You should go there anyway: it's a great nature preserve!)

BLUE DICKS
Dipterostemon capitatus

A flower of spring grasslands, this plant also has an edible bulb.

* One-to-two-foot stalk; grass-like leaves

* Common in open areas, especially after fires

* Blue, purple, pink, or white flowers

* Native to California, Mexico, and the Southwest

FIRE-FOLLOWING MINI-POTATOES

From February into June, Sonoma's grasslands and oak woodlands glow with the blue, lavender, or white blossoms from this common and drought-tolerant plant. It has a tall, thin stalk and long, thin, grass-like leaves. Other names include brodiaea ("bro-dee-ya") and Indian potato. The "dicks" part comes from a Greek word for technical features of the flower. (The technical names later changed, but the common name lives on.)

This plant does well in open or recently disturbed habitats, and after a fire there may be entire hillsides covered with it. Hidden underground is the edible bulb called a corm, which is about the size of a baby carrot. From grizzly bears to Pomo Indians, all of early California's original inhabitants liked to eat it. Acorns get lots of attention as an important food source, but historically this species was equally valuable. We will get a better chance to explore the ecology of blue dicks on page 161, when we go on a hike with our Native American guide, Clint McKay.

CALIFORNIA BUCKEYE
Aesculus californica

The buckeye loses its leaves earlier than other trees, making it look dead early in fall. But it is the first to green up in spring, looking very much alive again. Then it flares with vibrant, candle-like white blossoms that attract many butterflies. The blossoms are so vivid, you can spot a tree on a hillside even at freeway speeds.

* Umbrella-shaped, midsize tree

* Loses leaves in late summer: bare branches up to six months of year

* Flares with vibrant white and pale pink blossoms early in the spring

* Toxic, large chestnut-shaped "buckeye" seeds—do not eat!

THE BEAT OF A DIFFERENT DRUMMER

Buckeyes are midsize trees of forest, hillside, and river bottom. By the time the rains stop in early summer, buckeyes start shedding their leaves (a characteristic ecologists call "drought-deciduous"). Winter brings bare trunks and empty branches that can look ghostly in December fog. As early as February you will see the green return, and the cycle renews itself.

The name *buckeye* refers to the seeds that this tree produces in fall, which look like a deer's eye when the fruit splits open, revealing the seed. These shiny, large seeds that look like chestnuts are hard to miss when they lie on the ground eager to sprout. All parts of the tree, the seed included, are toxic to humans. It is fine to pick one up, but don't eat it.

Native bees visit blossoms without harm, but buckeye nectar is toxic to nonnative honey bees.

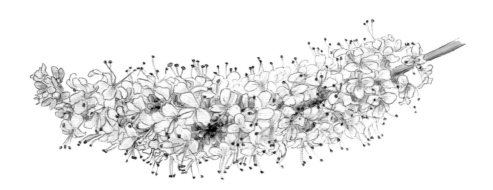

CALIFORNIA POPPY
Eschscholzia californica

From meadows to vacant lots to roadsides, our state flower paints spring and summer days bright orange. The flowers do not like wind, cold days, or dark nights, so remain furled during inclement conditions.

* Flowers very orange, sometimes with yellow at the tips

* Blooms protected by conical "dunce cap"

* Annual flower, blooming most (but not all) springs

* Flowers close up in cold weather

LOVED AT HOME, EXPORTED ABROAD

If the word *orange* could somehow be made to represent an even more saturated, more ultravibrant amount of orange-ness, then it might just barely be adequate to describe the rich orange intensity of a field of California poppies. These annual (and sometimes perennial) flowers can show up as early as January and last as long as late summer, but

The poppy grown for opium was originally native to the Mediterranean and is not related to our plant. Even tiny bees can't get high off this kind.

their peak is often late spring. They respond to rain (more is good) and other triggers that are not fully known; you can expect them most years but not all, or at least not in abundance.

The plant itself is low and feathery, about twelve to twenty-four inches tall, and varies from grass green to a delicate sage green. This poppy has been exported abroad and planted in gardens, as well as being intentionally spread along road berms, until the wild and the cultivated intermingle freely. The flowers attract bees and butterflies, and are also pollinated by beetles. Looking closely inside a blossom often lets you spot multiple insect species jostling for a turn at the nectar buffet.

Wild poppies are usually but not always orange. Some can be darker or lighter than typical, and some are even yellow, beige, or white.

COAST LIVE OAK
Quercus agrifolia

Giver of shade and bearer of acorns, coast live oak is one of the most essential members of the oak-grassland community.

* Thick-trunked, tent-canopied paterfamilias of the California land-scape

* Evergreen with small, holly-like leaves, curled inward

* Both inland and coastal (though not directly on ocean's edge)

* Drought and fire resistant

WHERE WILL *YOU* BE IN 250 YEARS?

Oaks can live for hundreds of years. More than two hundred species of insects use this oak as a host plant, and not just acorn woodpeckers and scrub-jays harvest the nuts, but deer graze them, as did, in the not-so-distant past, grizzly bears. One study found that 25 percent of all land mammals in California eat acorns, and of course, California's Native Americans famously harvested acorns. The term *synchronized masting* means that the oaks "talk" to each other through chemical cues, so that trees over a wide area know to produce acorn crops at the same time. This floods the system with seeds, ensuring that some can survive to grow into new oaks later on.

The leaves are small and curled; as docents often tell students, "If it floats like a boat, it's a coast live oak."

COAST REDWOOD
Sequoia sempervirens

Bristlecone pines and giant sequoias may be older, but no tree in the world grows taller than the coast redwood. Native to California; it can occur in pure stands or mixed with other species.

* Tall trunk, brown bark (not bright red like sequoia or incense cedar)

* Needles are flattened and about a half-inch long

* One-inch cones, crisscrossed with a diamond pattern

* Tallest redwood is over 380 feet (exact location kept hidden)

HOW TO LIVE TO BE VERY TALL AND VERY OLD

Redwoods have been present in California for twenty million years. They have evolved the perfect mix of defenses, with thick bark that is resistant to fire, insects, and disease, and a shade tolerance that allows it to grow slowly but steadily even in a crowded understory. One water source is condensed fog. Its usual lifespan is 500–700 years, but more than 2,000 years is possible. The wood was irresistible to commercial interests, so during the nineteenth century the Sonoma region was called "the Redwood Empire"—not for what was preserved but for what was lost. Luckily, redwoods are growing back and can be found in many parks and preserves.

Besides looking cool and being inspiring and providing nesting platforms for everything from marbled murrelets to condors, coast redwoods are really good at sequestering carbon. More redwood trees will mean slower climate change.

Armstrong Redwoods State Natural Reserve has trees that include the Colonel Armstrong Tree (over fourteen hundred years old) and the Parson Jones Tree, 310 feet tall. The limiting factor on height may be the physics of water: the pressure needed to lift water from root to crown reaches a point where the system just can't work anymore.

A mature redwood weighs about 6,000 tons—thirty times more than a blue whale.

COMMON MANZANITA
Arctostaphylos manzanita

Red bark, green leaves, and wide, bush-like shape—those features combine to help us identify a manzanita. It is never as tall as our other red tree, the Pacific madrone. Bears and coyotes love the manzanita's fall berries.

* Large bush (up to the size of a small tree)
* Trunk and branches twist up from central base
* Red and gray bark in barber-pole swirls
* Oval leaves; dinky, urn-shaped flowers; dark berries

BEAR BERRIES AND BABY APPLES

Can we name manzanita the de facto "state plant"? After all, 58 of the 60 world species are found here, and manzanita grows from coastal headlands up into the Sierra highlands. It blooms as early as January, a date appreciated by early arriving hummingbirds. In fact, if you walk along a trail of blooming manzanita in late winter, you may get dive-bombed by a male hummingbird guarding "his" nectar source. Manzanita do not need fire for seeds to germinate, but they can live hundreds of years, and their seeds remain viable for decades. When fire clears the ground and releases chemicals, the seeds are ready, and they often will sprout after the next big rainfall.

The small, dark berries ripen in late summer and are a favorite food for bears, foxes, and birds. The common name means "little apple," and the genus name comes from "bear berry." When hiking, you may find seed-filled scat claiming pride of place in the middle of the trail. It might be from a bear, or, as the manzanita would say, from "an all-wheel-drive seed dispersal device."

 Manzanita is part of the shrubland community called chaparral. The term comes from the Spanish word chaparro ("place of small trees") and has been in use since the 1840s.

DOUGLAS-FIR

Pseudotsuga menziesii

The Douglas-fir is a tall, loose-limbed, spruce-like conifer that occurs in pure stands or mixed forests.

- Gray, vertically fissured bark

- Tall enough to be confused with redwoods

- Dangling cones have overlapping scales and fluttery tufts

- Needles emerge around all sides of the twig

TO KEEP TREES FROM BURNING (WE SHOULD BURN MORE TREES)

The Douglas-fir—sometimes just called "Doug fir" by foresters—is a tall, rain-loving forest tree whose coastal range stretches from British Columbia to Sonoma. There are also populations in the Sierra and the Rockies. Trees grow 350 years in the wild and can be the tallest nonredwoods in the forest. In the American West, this commonly harvested tree is used for everything from Christmas trees to cathedral beams. On the taxonomy lists, it does not quite fit in. It is not a true fir, not a true pine, not a true hemlock, and yet has elements of each. None of that confusion bothers wildlife—the seeds are eaten by squirrels and the needles by Sonoma tree voles; the voles in turn sustain spotted owls.

Fire suppression has let this species take over oak groves and other places where it was not originally present, which creates conditions for hotter, fiercer fires than were historically common. To stop these megafires, it would better to thin out Douglas-fir with controlled burns. It is a great tree—it just has been allowed to grow places it doesn't really belong.

Local naturalists help young visitors identify Douglas-fir cones by likening the outer scales to the feet and tales of tiny mice trying to hide inside the cones.

DUF

DOUGLAS IRIS
Iris douglasiana

This is a tall, thin-leaved flower that to a novice looks like an orchid (but isn't). Insects love it.

* Purple flowers (also can be white, blue, or pink)
* Whole plant up to two feet tall and two feet wide
* Forests, edges, and grasslands
* Mostly low elevation, coastal

THE PERFECT RESTAURANT

With a long blooming period (February to July), Douglas iris brings color to the coastal prairies and mixed evergreen forests throughout Sonoma County. Its wide, welcoming flowers come in many hues, from white to a deep indigo to pinks and lavenders in between. Irises support many beneficial insects, and one botanist describes iris flowers as the perfect restaurant. It has three important retail features: good signage (the large, colorful petals to attract bees), plenty of parking (the lower petals with wide landing strips), and great food (the delicious nectar).

Douglas iris is named after the same Scottish botanist who is remembered in name of the fir tree in the previous entry. It is perennial and tends to grow in patches as it spreads from underground stems called rhizomes. If you find a favorite iris patch, chances are it will be there year after year, quietly expanding.

FIELD MUSTARDS
Brassica spp.

These widespread and aggressive weeds are attractive, but they compete with native plants.

* Abundant in vacant lots and fields—you rarely see just one

* Thin, tall stems and small yellow flower heads

* Leaves "grab" the stalk, like two hands wrapping around a stick

* Other look-alike species include the black mustard, *B. nigra*

GOOD-BYE YELLOW BRICK ROAD

Without fail, vineyards in Sonoma and Napa turn a bright sunny yellow in February as the various species of field mustard bloom. It's a sight that makes visitors pull over and get out their cameras to capture the alluring color. We like more than just looking at it. The mustard family includes many vegetables, including broccoli, cabbage, turnips, brussels sprouts, and of course mustard seed, which is the source of the yellow sauce on hotdogs.

Mustards—as beautiful as they are—are nevertheless an invasive species. They flourish in disturbed land, so look for them in vacant lots, and not (we hope) in the center of a redwood forest. All species of mustard have a unique feature—the flowers of all these plants have four petals arranged in a cross-like formation. Consequently, this family of plants used to be called the Cruciferae—"like a crucifix." It is thought that our current mustards were brought by the Spanish padres who seeded their way north on the Camino Real, thus marking a golden trail during spring—a kind of map for the journey home to Mexico.

PACIFIC MADRONE
Arbutus menziesii

This red-barked tree has bright green leaves. The main trunk can be single or multiple. It is a medium-size tree in most woodlands.

* 30–60 feet tall (up to 100 feet)
* Large, lightly serrated leaf is shiny green above, dull silver below
* Slopes or oak-filled canyons, mixed evergreen forests, open chaparral
* In spring, covered with drooping clusters of small, white, cup-shaped flowers

HAPPY BIRDS AND COOL HANDS

Madrones are in the same family as manzanita. Both have orange-to-maroon bark and sweet white flowers shaped like urns, but madrones are usually taller, and on a madrone, the bark peels off in thin layers, often revealing pale green bark underneath. Fruit appears in fall in the form of soft orange balls about the size of marbles. They are edible, but not tasty—at least not to us. Doves, pigeons, robins, and deer—everybody else likes them just fine.

This is sometimes called the "refrigerator tree," because in summer the trunk feels cool to the touch. Technically, it is not "colder" than other trees; you are feeling the flow of water just under the skin of the tree, which pulls heat away from the surface of your own hand. (Most other trees are too furrowed for this to work.)

Unfortunately, both madrone and bay laurels are carriers of a fungus-like pathogen that causes Sudden Oak Death, or SOD. This is a serious problem in Sonoma and other coastal counties in California. Madrones are not generally susceptible to SOD, but they can pass it on to other trees. Wet winters spread the disease more easily than dry years, providing one of the few upsides to a drought cycle.

PACIFIC POISON OAK
Toxicodendron diversilobum

A common plant in woodlands and chaparral, poison oak can cause a burning rash. Use caution near it—but enjoy the wildlife it attracts.

- ❋ "Leaves of three, leave it be"

- ❋ Can be a low bush, climbing vine, or robust shrub

- ❋ Often a few leaves are red or yellow, even in spring

- ❋ For some, it gives an intense rash; if unsure, go around

THE "UNLESS" PLANT

Poison oak deserves every inch of its bad rap as a drives-you-mad-with-scratching rash giver, and you should avoid touching it with hands or boots, *unless*—

Well, unless you're one of the lucky ones who can't "catch" poison oak because the oils don't happen to react with your skin. Or unless you're a robin or a waxwing or a bluebird and the berries are ripe. Or unless you are a browsing deer: deer and cattle can eat the berries and leaves and not have a bad reaction.

The solution for us humans is to learn the shape. Green- and red-lobed leaves cluster in groups of three, hence the rhyme. The edges of the leaf are smooth, unlike the prickly edges of the blackberry bushes often growing nearby. The full plant can be a bush or a sprawling vine, and it typically is an understory plant, especially along creeks. It tolerates full sun, too; all the hikes in this book have the possibility for poison oak. The berries sustain lots of wildlife, so this is a natural and important part of the plant community. Celebrate it; don't curse it

 Only humans, guinea pigs, and monkeysreact to poison oak. Almost all other wildlife does fine with it.

SKY LUPINE
Lupinus nanus

This is a common, annual, blue-purple wildflower found throughout oak woodlands, grasslands, and open areas. It blooms in March and April. Pretty!

* Purple blossoms on tall stalks

* Total plant is one to two feet tall

* Open slopes, chaparral clearings

* Coastal ranges and the Sierra foothills

HOW TO SWITCH THE "VACANCY" SIGN TO "NO VACANCY"

Stand downwind of a lupine field in March and breathe in the distinct aroma of grape soda—*ahhh*. Even better, it is often found with popcorn flower, California buttercup, California poppy, spring vetch, and other blooming wonders.

With their tall, many-flowered stems and welcoming leaves shaped like a palm, lupines attract pollinators, especially bees. You can tell which flowers have already been visited by bees by their color. Sky lupine has a white spot on its top petal (the "banner petal"). Bees look for this spot to find nectar-rich flowers. Once the flower has been pollinated, the spot turns to a darker magenta. Thus the bees can avoid flowers with depleted nectar.

Lupines (and vetch and all clovers) "fix" nitrogen in the soil. Even though 80 percent of our air is made up of nitrogen, it is in a molecular form that is not useable to plants. Specialized bacteria need to convert it to a form that plants can use, and lupines host that bacteria in their roots. Some people call this conversion process "green manure," since the growing plants themselves enrich the soil.

SPRING VETCH
Vicia sativa

A nonnative, pink-flowered plant, spring vetch climbs up other plants and has ant bodyguards.

* Small pink flowers

* Thin-leafed, slender, vine-like plant

* To house the seeds, creates a two-inch pea pod

* Open fields, disturbed areas (often with other flowers)

LAZY GUARDS AND ACTIVE ANTS

Spring vetch bears its bright pink, purple, or reddish flowers on delicate vines that twine their way up other plants. It is not native to California, but has been here long enough (and has been spread widely enough) to have become naturalized. It is found in other states too, from Alaska to Florida. As with sky lupine, vetch helps soil by hosting bacteria that convert nitrogen in the air to a form usable by plants. The sister plant, winter vetch, does the same thing.

Vetch plants have a cool mutualist relationship with ants. The flowers have tiny glands called "extrafloral nectaries" that make a sweet nectar that is sought after by ants. The ants are so fond of their floral treats that they patrol constantly, protecting the host from invasion by other would-be herbivores. Next time you see a vetch flower, look closely to spot its vigilant ant bodyguards.

STICKY MONKEY-FLOWER
Diplacus aurantiacus

Monkey-flower is a tall bush that produces orchid-shaped yellow flowers. Hummingbirds (and botanists) love it.

* Three to four feet tall

* Orangey-yellow flowers with a "face"

* Shiny, linear leaves

* Chaparral, evergreen forest, oak woodland

BEES, BUTTERFLIES, AND ALL-SUMMER BLOOMS

Sticky monkey-flower is Sonoma's "Orange Dreamsicle" perennial. Blooming from March through August (and even longer in some years), this delightful shrub displays its juicy orange-and-cream face in chaparral, mixed forest, and oak woodlands. Related to other monkey-flower species, it has a characteristic two-lipped structure. Emerging from two orange flower lips is the female part of the flower—the stigma—where pollen must land or be deposited in order to fertilize the flower. If you touch it with your finger, it will immediate close up, hoping to have gleaned some pollen grains. Do it just once or twice, then stop, or better yet, stay still while a bee or fly or other pollinator deposits pollen on that delicate structure.

When the flower is not being poked by curious botanists, this plant's usual pollinators are bees and hummingbirds. Sticky monkey-flower is also a host plant for butterflies, especially checkerspots and buckeyes. The plants outlive the butterflies by a ratio of about a hundred-to-one. A typical buckeye (104) spends a week or two as an egg, two to four weeks as a caterpillar, then goes into its chrysalis stage. That lasts one to two weeks.

The emerged adult usually only lives a few more weeks past that. Since the monkey-flower is an evergreen perennial, it does not just bloom and die. That means that a single plant may host many, many generations of butterflies. On behalf of the butterflies, let us be the first to say, "Thank you."

 The name comes from the shape of the flower, which (to some people) looks like the face of a grinning monkey.

TOYON
Heteromeles arbutifolia

This is a large, drought-tolerant shrub with red berries in winter: the "Christmas Berry" bush.

* 6–10 feet tall; 4–5 feet around (can be taller and wider)

* White flowers in summer; loads of small red fruit in winter

* Oval, leathery leaves, two to four inches long

* Can tolerate droughts and fires . . . up to a point

MAGICAL CHRISTMAS BUSH

This is a very bushy bush, tall and robust, found along streams, on chaparral hillsides, and inside the forest. It provides sustenance to vertebrates and invertebrates alike all year long. Summer flowers attract butterflies and other insects, and in fall and winter, as the berries mature, they are eaten (and redistributed with an added dollop of fertilizer) by bears, coyotes, robins, mockingbirds, waxwings, thrushes, squirrels, and just about any other bird or critter out and about in the late-season forest. Unless you have a particularly odd palette (or unless you cook it up with sugar into cobbler), the fruit is too astringent for humans. But if instead of eating it you plant toyon around your house, then you can help wildlife and have a busy yard all year long.

One source posits that this species, once established and in a normal fire environment, can live as long as an oak tree. No baseline data is available to confirm or deny, so for now, we will agree. Come back and ask us again in 290 years.

 Toyon is the Spanish version of the word given to this plant by the Ohlone people.

VALLEY OAK
Quercus lobata

This is a grand and admired tree of interior hills and valleys; it has larger, more "fingered" leaves than the coast live oak's.

- Mature trees have a large, spreading crown
- Tips of branches often "droop" (like weeping willows)
- Leaves are two to four inches long and deeply lobed
- The large, one-to-two-inch acorns have bumpy caps

TREE OF LIFE

Oak trees are perhaps the single most iconic element of the Sonoma landscape. There are ten species of oaks here, but this one outshines the others. Besides living for hundreds of years and having the largest acorns, the valley oak is the tallest American oak tree and also one of the most easily recognized. The spreading shape umbrellas out from a stout trunk, which can be six feet across. Sometimes the branches arch down all the way to the ground. A healthy valley oak can survive periodic fire, so long as fire does not come back too frequently or burn with unusual intensity.

Oak galls look like wooden apples. You can spot them on the ends of branches or scattered on the ground. They're not a natural fruit, but develop because a wasp tricks the tree into making the "apple" as a home for its eggs and larvae. Gall shapes vary by wasp, and to see several examples, look on page 179.

Valley oaks are water lovers and tend to grow in rich soils along rivers and streams. But don't be surprised if you find them away from streams or at higher elevations; they are very adaptable. There were once more of them, as is true for many things, from grizzlies to condors. We can celebrate the ones that are left, though. A local music teacher described this species as the "Beethoven of oaks"—bold, strong, and transcending all its rivals.

Contrary to expectation, valley oak wood does not make good timber. (One pioneer nickname was "mush oak.")

BUMBLE BEES
Bombus spp.

The bumble bee group includes any of twenty-six native species of large, fuzzy, yellow-and-black bees. They live in burrows and are essential for pollinating wildflowers and crops, performing an important service for free.

* Half-inch to one-inch long

* Yellow and black; "fuzzy" or "furry"

* Loud, buzzing flight

THE QUEEN IS DEAD (LONG LIVE THE QUEEN)

Our story starts in spring. Pregnant queens have spent the winter burrowed underground, hibernating. They emerge and find a mouse burrow or other hole in the ground as a new nest site. The queen uses abdominal glands to create wax pots to store nectar, and she also lays the first crop of eggs, housing them inside recently gathered pollen balls. As an army of one, she incubates the first brood, forages for food for them and herself, and defends the nest.

The hatchlings end up as workers. They now forage and guard, and the queen stays in the nest, laying eggs and tending successive broods. *Bombus* colonies usually contain only about fifty bees and are smaller than honey-bee colonies. Unlike most native bees, which are solitary, the bumble bee is social. By the end of summer, a colony produces males and females—both fertile—that leave the nest to mate. In the fall, the males die off, but the mated females—future queens—spend their time eating and storing fat so that they can hibernate over winter.

SMALL, MEDIUM, OR LARGE

Bee species vary in size. A small-tongued kind cannot reach into a flower designed for a longer-tongued kind. Some get around this by cheating—drilling into a flower from the outside, then poaching nectar without providing pollination in return. (Some tropical birds do this too.)

There are sixteen hundred species of bees in California. A large, all-black bee, slow and loud, is not a bumble bee but a female carpenter bee, so named because it chews its way into dead wood and fence posts to make its nest chambers. The golden-hued males are sometimes called teddy bear bees. They do not have a stinger.

Native bees in general are not to be feared. According to Gordon Frankie of UC Berkeley, "Native bees have a list of three things they are interested in: pollen, nectar, and sex. You're not on that list; don't worry about getting stung!" So just follow the Golden Rule and don't poke them in their nest.

A bee is not a wasp (and a wasp is not a bee); for more on that distinction, please see yellowjackets, 106.

CABBAGE WHITE
Pieris rapae

As the name promises, the cabbage white is a common garden butterfly that is white or a yellow version of white.

* Small and fluttery, going flower to flower on a buoyant but erratic journey
* Yellow-white with smudgy black wingtips and one or two black dots
* Wingspan just under two inches
* Spring, summer, and fall on roadsides and in meadows, yards, gardens

OLD SPECIES, NEW ARRIVAL

"White" refers to the butterfly's color, and "cabbage" tells us what the caterpillar eats—any plant, wild or cultivated, from the mustard and cabbage families. These are Old World plants and this is an Old World butterfly, accidentally introduced to Canada in 1860 and now spread throughout the Lower 48 and Hawaii. (Alaska has a native "white," but not this species.)

The small and delightful cabbage white can brighten any afternoon, yet one agriculture source complains that "the cabbage worm is a dangerous invasive species." Their phrasing reveals their bias: nobody loves worms, but most of us are quite fond of butterflies.

GET OFF HERE!

Flowers want to be pollinated and butterflies want to find nectar, but how can the two puzzle pieces find each other, given the grand cacophony of stimuli that most environments present? It seems that the cabbage white uses multiple clues to figure out where to go. The first is visual: they are attracted to things that are purple, blue, or yellow. The second is smell: the plant can emit chemical clues that will attract insect pollinators. The third is experience, as they learn which plants on which streets have been good to visit in the past.

We now are beginning to explore the role of ultraviolet light in the animal world. To attract butterflies, the flower paints the target area with UV markings, which are not visible to us, since our range of vision is too narrow. The cabbage white can see it though, and reacts appropriately. It is as if the flower has hoisted a giant sign high above the interstate, "Last gas for 50 miles—exit now!"

This is one butterfly that can be seen anywhere and everywhere. One website even points out that this "is one of just a few species of butterfly that can be reliably identified while driving 70 mph."

CALIFORNIA SISTER
Adelpha californica

This oak woodland butterfly has black wings enhanced by orange circles and white stripes. To some early viewers, the contrasting black and white recalled a nun's habit, hence "sister."

* Strong flyer, from treetops to streamside and all points in between

* 2.5–4 inches; large and showy; attracted to rotting fruit

* Orange circle does not extend past wing edge (unlike a species called an admiral)

NATURE, HERE WE COME

This species can be seen in town, but prefers oaks and riparian woods. The primary host plant for the caterpillar is canyon live oak. Related sisters are in oak forests in Arizona and Mexico, and the other members of the genus extend their ranges all the way to the bottom of South America. One of the fun things about travel is seeing the other parts of an ecological continuum that you know from home. Like tasting the *terroir* in a new wine, noticing how color patterns vary across climates and geographies enhances away-from-home hiking and photography.

HOW TO SEE BUTTERFLIES AND MOTHS
(AND GRASSHOPPERS AND LADYBUGS)

Butterflies are fun to watch, and among many other admirable traits, they come out at a reasonable hour of the day. If it is spring, look for a flowering tree such as a buckeye, whose blossoms attract butterflies. To get the best views, a pair of binoculars helps. The "power" (8× or 10×) matters less than whether that model focuses closely or not. Try a few to see what feels balanced in your hands. No binos? Cell-phone pictures can be nearly as good.

This is a species that is good for binocular study because it "puddles." It needs minerals, and one way to get them is by licking damp soil (or horse urine or bear scat . . . see page 194). As this species and other butterflies "puddle up" around a stream edge or on damp, bare earth, they generally are easier to see than when zagging flower to flower. If you stand still and stay back a bit (standing in the shade helps), they usually will ignore you.

If your binoculars focus closely enough, you can study exquisite insect details, such as the balls of pollen on the hind leg of a bee or the tiny daubs of orange on a California sister's wing edge. Being quiet and still helps, but if the creature in question flies off, give it a few minutes, and it will probably be back.

COMMON BUCKEYE

Junonia coenia

The buckeye is an attractive, easily noticed butterfly, with obvious eyespots on its busy wings.

* Midsize: not small, not huge

* Brown with orange stripes and blue-and-tan circles

* Open areas: fields, meadows, gardens (sits directly on ground)

* Spring, summer, fall (rare in winter)

OK, "EYE" CAN SEE YOU

Imagine you are watching a flock of birds at the feeder. You need a better view, so you reach for your binoculars, slooowly lifting them up. Just as they reach eye level, the desired bird flies off. What happened? Option (A), it was going to fly anyway; (B), the motion startled it; or (C), two big black shining eyes—the objective lenses—looked like the eyes of a predator, and that scared it off. On the birding forums, (C) gets a lot of votes.

The buckeye wants to be those binoculars. And to emphasize the wing-eyes even more, the largest eyespots are framed in pale commas, which curl up like cat ears. "Don't try to eat me—I can see you!"

Adults spend their time looking for nectar or probing a stream bank for salt or tasting the oozing juices of a roadkilled deer. Male buckeye butterflies drink from rotting food sources that the females ignore.

Once mated, females lay small green eggs, one at a time, like a row of rice grains the color of watermelons. Local host plants for the eggs include monkey-flower and plantain. Next comes a caterpillar, which goes through four molt cycles and crawls under a leaf, where it attaches itself with a small amount of silk and forms a J shape. Its skin then dries and splits, revealing a chrysalis underneath. When it emerges two weeks later, it is an adult buckeye.

A BUCKEYE ON A BUCKEYE

In our area, adult food plants include coyote brush and California buckeye (73). If the buckeye tree in question is growing in the yard of somebody from Ohio, you can see a buckeye on a buckeye hosted by a Buckeye.

 The eggs of the Common Buckeye are green with pale stripes and would look like baby watermelons, except they are only 1 millimeter long.

COMMON YELLOWJACKET
Vespula pensylvanica

Wasps look like bees only more so: longer, sleeker, glossier—more hunter and less gatherer.

* Bee colored, but note cinched waist and back-swept wings

* Nests in colonies underground

* Eats both nectar and meat

* Careful: can have a powerful sting!

THE HOLE-IN-THE-WALL GANG

This wasp is a ground-dwelling species, often using a former rodent burrow, but attics and walls get exploited as well. Different species of yellowjackets in our area also build aerial nests about the size of a football that hang from trees.

In early spring, an overwintering queen locates a nest site and lays the first set of eggs. The nest chamber is built out of paper-mâché, created from wood pulp. New workers have to locate more fiber for nest chambers, track down sources of nectar and water (your open can of soda pop will do nicely), hunt for meat, tend the larvae, clean the nest, defend the nest, and squabble with other workers. (The term "mauling" comes up often in the literature.) Populations per nest range from a few hundred to twenty thousand. By summer's end, the queens-to-be are pregnant and ready to burrow underground, and thus the cycle can resume next year.

CICADAS, THE OTHER WHITE MEAT

Yellowjackets are both nectar gatherers and predators, and in their hunting phase, potential prey includes flies, moths, grasshoppers, cockroaches, cicadas, bees, spiders, and even other yellowjackets. They do scavenge carrion, and to them, that includes the charred bits of fat on your barbecue grill or even the fresh hamburger itself. Swat at them carefully, since wasps are easy to anger and hard to appease, and they can indeed sting multiple times in a row. (As can most bees, other than honey bees.)

HOW TO TELL THE "YELLOW-AND-BLACKS" APART

Because they have similar colors and similar reputations for stinging people, wasps and bees get mixed together in most people's minds. Wasps eat meat (some of the time), and bees eat pollen and nectar (all of the time). Wasps are usually long, slender, and wasp waisted; bees are blunt and round. The two groups fold their wings differently at rest—wasps' are more swept back. Wasps are glossy or at least hairless; bees can look shaggy or fuzzy. Both groups usually have yellow-and-black stripes, but then so do hover flies, so color alone won't be enough. Instead, look at structure, fuzziness, and behavior.

A hornet is a large, black-and-white wasp, though the terms *wasp* and *hornet* are often used interchangeably by the public.

DARKLING BEETLES
Eleodes spp.

Darkling beetles are solo scavengers, walking trails and forest floors. If threatened, they can stop, lock their back legs, and poke their bottoms up in the air. Next comes an oily, noxious spray that can jet out twelve inches.

* 1–1.5 inches long
* Shiny black and hard shelled
* Scavenger that is active day or night
* If threatened, shoots out noxious spray

NAMES ARE SLIPPERY THINGS

A lot of Western hikers call this large black beetle a stink bug. Yet that same term also applies to a recently arrived Asian insect, *Halyomorpha halys*, or the brown marmorated stink bug. The Asian stink bug is much smaller and browner than a darkling beetle and is shaped like an arrowhead. It seeks out everything from apricots to soy beans and causes millions of dollars of crop damage. That is not the insect illustrated here: one name, two different critters.

Calling "our" stink bug a darkling beetle not only clears up that confusion but is more elegant, even Victorian. Literature majors may remember a Thomas Hardy poem, "The Darkling Thrush," about how a bird brings hope to a weary villager at the end of a gloomy day. The word *darkling* has seen a small revival; there are half a dozen recent Darkling characters in science fiction novels and comics.

CYCLES OF RECYCLING

Darkling beetles patrol the ground, eating dead insects, rotting leaves, seeds, fungus, and anything else they come across. The dung beetle clan performs a similar duty, with a focus on animal waste. Besides being good recyclers, darkling beetles serve us another way. They have a four-part life cycle: egg, larva, pupa, and adult. The mealworms sold in pet stores are not worms but the larvae of darkling beetles. Dried, they also become fish food.

 There are 400,000 known beetle species worldwide (and perhaps twice that amount still to be described).

FLAME SKIMMER
Libellula saturata

This is a conspicuous flame-red dragonfly with clear wings, usually seen over or near water.

- Two to three inches long (body) and wide (wings)
- Males are bright rust orange, including eyes and wing veins
- Females and immatures are plainer, browner
- Spring and summer, perched on reeds or patrolling a pond

VERY, VERY SMALL DINOSAURS

In their own way, dragonflies are *T. rexes*. After hatching from eggs that were spaced apart (so they don't all get eaten and so the hatchlings don't eat each other), 80 percent of a dragonfly's one- or two-year life span is spent underwater. This is called the nymph stage. Nymphs look like aquatic earwigs, and they are fierce predators of beetle and mosquito larvae, their fellow nymphs, worms, fish, and tadpoles. They practice ambush hunting, using extendable mouthparts. When a potential meal passes, the nymph's lower jaw will shoot out with lightning speed. Zap—gotcha! They are one of the top predators under the pond's surface.

As summer approaches, nymphs crawl onto a reed to create a shell and turn into a flying adult. They now look (and act) like regular dragonflies, and males try to control a stretch of pond that they hope females will find attractive. Location, location, location: the females want the best site for egg laying, and select males based on territory, not their good looks. As adults, both sexes remain predators and consume 10 to 15 percent of their weight each day. They hunt anything that flies past, including ants, bees, flies, midges, moths, termites, and other dragonflies. They mate on the wing, then the female lays her eggs, and so the cycle continues.

MEADOWHAWKS AND RUBYSPOTS

Once you start to notice flame skimmers, you can see them all over (even parking lots), and from there, watch for blue ones, green ones, and some of the other reds, such as the neon skimmer or cardinal meadowhawk or desert firetail, which despite the name occurs all the way north to Mendocino County.

Damselflies are related to dragonflies, but are smaller and slimmer. They hold their wings parallel to the body, while dragonfly wings extend out on each side, like transparent airplane wings.

HARVESTER ANT
Veromessor andrei

These ants are soil-enriching subterranean supercolonists. They harvest seeds (and some insects) and build inverted condo towers underground. Without them, a lot of soil would still be dirt.

* Half-inch long

* Red body with black abdomen

* Nest opening is a hole in the ground that is surrounded by duff

* Nests often in the middle of hiking trails

I'M HUNGRY, PLEASE BARF ON ME

Ants aerate the soil, speed the decomposition of organic material, enhance drainage, and bring improved, mulch-fortified material back up to the surface, where it is spread by wind, rain, and their own to-ing and fro-ing.

Some colonies last many years, but each season a new brood of queens sets out to start new colonies. When a queen starts a colony, she reabsorbs her wing muscles for energy while she raises her first brood of worker ants. (She can't yet eat.) At first, workers will all be female. Some gather food, mostly seeds that are then stored in special chambers. Some tidy it up underground, some defend the nest, some tend to the queen, and some take care of the larvae in special nurseries. In time, the nest will grow to be ten feet deep (or more), with many layers and chambers, resembling a skyscraper turned upside down.

The larvae eat seeds and regurgitate them for adults, who cannot eat the seeds directly. The husks from shelled seeds, soil from excavations, and bodies of ants who have died belowdecks all get carried up to the surface. As the colony matures, the queen lays a few special eggs that will become males and a few that will become daughter queens. Both groups have wings. Together, the males and future queens exit the colony and fly away; after mating, the males will die. They have just that one job to do, so let's hope they enjoy doing it.

HOW DO YOU HARVEST THE HARVESTERS?

Western fence lizards can eat ants, and you sometimes see their tiny black pellets in the duff around the ant colony entrances—not seeds, lizard poop. Yet it's hard to eat ant, given that ants sting and bite and contain formic acid.

For one desert species, the horned lizard (also called "horny toads"), the secret is mucous. As the lizard eats ants, glands in the back of the throat coat each ant in a neutralizing ball of mucous and send it down the hatch. With that clever trick, the inedible becomes very edible.

MOURNING CLOAK
Nymphalis antiopa

This is a handsome but dark butterfly, named mourning (not morning) because of the somber color.

- Four-inch wingspan
- Wing is maroon-brown with cream edges and blue dots
- Can live a full year (usually summer to summer)
- The older the butterfly, the more ragged the wings

ALTITUDINAL MIGRATION

In California, the mourning cloak has several patterns of behavior. In the (relatively) warm lowlands such as Sonoma, they can thrive by being locavores. They like riparian streams and oak woodlands. Mourning cloaks in Central California migrate to the higher elevations in summer (up to seven thousand feet) and return to the lowlands in winter.

This species also successfully hibernates, even in very cold areas. They have a natural kind of antifreeze in their blood and can endure harsh weather. As cold, wet weather approaches, a solo butterfly finds a protected nook such as a gap under loose bark, a dense cluster of leaves, or the corner of an old barn, and hunkers down until spring. In the Midwest they can even emerge while there is still snow on the ground. Several butterfly researchers report finding mourning cloak butterflies hibernating inside beer cans. If there is a bit of beer left over, they apparently like it even better. Because they can overwinter, mourning cloaks are often the first butterflies we see in Sonoma in early spring.

SAP, NOT ROSES

Many adult butterflies hover over flowers, hoping to suck up nectar. Mourning cloaks show less interest in flowers or even rotting fruit than do most other butterflies, and instead "graze" tree trunks, looking for sap. This may ooze from natural wounds in the trunk or come out of the holes drilled by woodpeckers and sapsuckers. You probably have seen these marks: horizontal rows of drill marks (called "sapwells"), sometimes encircling the entire trunk of a slim birch or ornamental pear. The sapsuckers eat the sap and also the insects attracted to the sap.

Of course, feeding on sap is a bit risky, given the stickiness problem. Prehistoric butterflies did sometimes get caught in sap and hence become fossilized in amber, so we know that butterflies similar to our modern species occurred as far back as the dinosaurs.

The spiky caterpillar is black with a row of red dots. Preferred host plants include willows, aspens, poplar, and cottonwoods. Caterpillars also eat the leaves of hackberry, hawthorn, birch, and fruitless mulberry.

This species occurs across most of Europe, but is a rare visitor to England, where it is called the Camberwell beauty.

PIPEVINE SWALLOWTAIL
Battus philenor

A vivid blue-black butterfly, the pipevine swallowtail has a unique one-to-one relationship with a host plant whose toxins protect it for life.

* Midnight blue with complementary orange wing spots—beautiful!

* Wingspan of three to four inches

* Meadows, streams, and open areas

* Toxic (or very distasteful) to birds that might want to eat it

APOSEMATIC COLORATION
(AND OTHER BIG WORDS FOR DULL PARTIES)

In every stage, the pipevine swallowtail is toxic to eat, and it wants you to know that. In California, this butterfly has only one host plant that it can use successfully, the California pipevine, which is also called Dutchman's pipe, after the shape of the flower. Toxic compounds in the plant accumulate in the caterpillar and are carried into adulthood, and then passed on to the eggs as well: the butterfly is born toxic, and each generation renews the defenses. Bright colors warn off anything trying to eat it.

That warning is called aposematic coloration. Other butterflies that have not eaten the poison evolve to use similar color patterns in an attempt to buy some safety as well; this visual poaching is called Batesian mimicry. Many animals try it, including the nonvenomous gopher snake, whose coloration mimics the brown, gray, and cream pattern of a rattlesnake.

THE BIRDS AND THE BEES

Since the young only can feed on one host plant, the male butterflies patrol those, hoping to use their iridescent splendiferousness as a way to convince nearby females that they are Mr. Right. Impregnated females then need to find the correct plant for laying eggs. Does Mom ever get it wrong? To quote one entomologist, "Oviposition mistakes by Lepidoptera are not uncommon." In other words, yes.

The "pipevine" part of the plant name refers to the bowl-shaped flower, which looks like a cross between a pitcher plant and the tobacco pipe in Magritte's "this is not a pipe" painting. The plant sometimes traps an arriving insect (usually a fungus fly) using downward-sloping hairs. Only after there has been a thorough exchange of pollen overnight does the flower open and release the fly—which will face the same ordeal at the next pipevine plant and the next one. Even insects have their Groundhog Days.

Adult pipevine swallowtails sip nectar from a range of our most common wildflowers, from blue dicks to thistles—anything pink or purple. Because it is so large and flies relatively slowly, the pipevine swallowtail is an excellent candidate for watching with binoculars.

BLACK BEAR
Ursus americanus

You probably will see tracks (or poo) and not the animal itself, but even a secondary encounter can be thrilling.

- Large (200–300 pounds; sometimes more)
- Can be black, brown, or cinnamon
- Eats everything from termites to berries to carrion
- Forests and meadows; can climb trees

NOT THE ONE ON THE FLAG

For most of California's history, if you were going to talk about bears, the species in question would be the grizzly bear, also called the brown bear. Larger than the black bear, it ended up on the flag but not in our ecology. The last one was seen in 1924. When they were here, they were common and gregarious, the way bears in Alaska might share a salmon run today. Grizzlies did appreciate California's salmon and steelhead, but also feasted on acorns and manzanita berries. They were much more common in the oak-savannah lowlands than the glacial peaks of the high Sierra, and if they were magically to reappear today, they would probably think that raiding a wine grape estate was the best thing ever.

With grizzlies gone, black bears could fill roles that their larger cousins had dominated. They eat everything, from Fido's dog food to a dead deer, but percentage-wise, most of their diet comes from plants and insects. Two or three cubs are born every second year on average, and cubs stay with Mom for a year and a half. We all know not to get between a mama bear and the little ones. Bears are much faster than they look: if you try to race a black bear, it will win.

Black bears live twenty years in the wild, and twice that is possible. Colors vary, even within the same litter, and the white "spirit bears" of British Columbia are black bears who just happen to have unusual coats.

We do know they are all around us. Black bears have been documented on game cameras many places in Sonoma County, including Sugarloaf Ridge State Park and Hood Mountain Regional Park, and they have been spotted in the vineyards of Alexander Valley.

WHAT IS THE RISK?

A bear might amble into town in the middle of the night, but it prefers to avoid people. Yes, they are around, but please don't let a fear of bears keep you off the trails. There have been no fatal bear attacks in California in at least a hundred years.

 Black bears can pick up scents from over a mile away.

BOBCAT
Lynx rufus

The bobcat is a midsize cat with an abbreviated ("bobbed") tail. Bigger than a housecat, more compact than a coyote, the bobcat never has a long flowing tail like a mountain lion.

- Brown with spots, though can be gray or tan
- Stubby tail (never bushy like a coyote's or long like a puma's)
- Patterned face has side-whiskers and pointed ears
- Dawn and dusk; meadows, edges, and fields

MIDSIZE AND DURABLE

A bobcat is three feet long and two feet high at the shoulder, and weighs twenty to thirty pounds, which means a bobcat is more like a midsize dog than a tabby cat. Look for their characteristic scat in the middle of trails, segmented like a giant tootsie roll and full of hair.

If they come across a dead livestock carcass, they will probably eat it—as would a coyote or bear or condor. That means they sometimes get unfairly labeled as sheep killers. Mostly bobcats are ambush predators, and in the case of pocket gophers or woodrats, their final pounce may include an acrobatic leap. A mule deer is a bit large for them to try to take down, but fawns are just the right size. Other prey include rabbits, mice, rats, birds, skunks, raccoons, feral cats, backyard koi in fish ponds, lizards, and, rarely, other bobcats.

Science calls animals in this size and role "mesopredators."

EVOLVING ATTITUDES

California used to allow bobcat trapping, as well as sport hunting by rifle, pistol, and bow. As recently as the 1980s, two thousand bobcats a year were being shot, and another eight thousand a year were trapped for their fur, and that was only counting animals legally taken and accounted for, not those killed by poachers. As of 2015, trapping stopped, and as of 2020, so did hunting. This allowed bobcats to fill in vacant pieces of wild landscape they used to inhabit.

At the same time, at least some bobcats show a tolerance of urbanization, and while they may not do as well as coyotes in exploiting the urban–wild edge zone, a few individuals can be quite visible and may even become YouTube stars by napping on porches or carrying kittens through a lane of traffic.

 Bobcats do not meow; they growl in a lion-like baritone

COYOTE
Canis latrans

This is the ultimate survivor, able to thrive despite our indifference and our persecution.

* Midsize social dog that yippy-yips after dark
* Tall ears, bushy tail, sandy coat mixed with gray
* Longer legs, more "wolf-like" body than gray fox
* Dawn, dusk, or nighttime; "pure" nature and also urban edges

INFINITELY EXPANDING MENU

Coyotes deserve our praise and admiration, since they inhabit almost as many kinds of habitat as we do, from Death Valley to the intertidal zone of rocky shorelines, and from the vineyards of Sonoma to the Mt. Whitney high country. Success comes from their remarkable social cohesion as family groups and packs and from their ability to exploit almost any kind of food—animal, vegetable, or mineral. That includes live prey like squirrels and voles, scavenged carrion, and such unexpected choices as cactus fruit, windfall apples, wine grapes, and caterpillars.

Coyotes weigh fifteen to thirty-five pounds, sometimes a bit more, and their tan and grizzled-gray coats blend into a variety of landscapes, from lichen-covered rocks to autumn's dried grass. Communication is by scent marking and howling. Packs are relatively small, with two to six adults, plus pups. Often the members are related. The pack defends a distinct territory, through which a solo, unaffiliated coyote passes quickly. In presettlement times, coyotes were predated by wolves, with whom they competed for scraps at bear kills. Now there are no wolves or grizzlies, but urban coyotes get hit by cars a lot, as we know from formal studies and as we can see for ourselves by driving for an hour on any California highway.

THE SOUND OF THE OLD WEST

Any votes on how we should transcribe their immense vocal range? They can yodel and yip and whine and chuff, for a total of a dozen or more distinct vocalizations. Howling carries half a mile or more and can be eerily ventriloqual. One will start, then another from the other side of the valley, and then a third, and then they all sound as though they are just ten yards away, hidden behind that bush over there. Some people love it, some are nervous, and everybody agrees: nothing else in nature sounds quite like it.

GRAY FOX
Urocyon cinereoargenteus

This attractive, thick-tailed fox is a regional specialty. Although they occur across much of North and Central America, here we are right in "fox central."

- Lower to the ground and thicker tailed than a coyote
- Cinnamon and iron gray, never sandy (coyote) or russet (red fox)
- Silent and solitary, though sometimes becomes used to people
- Agile: can scamper over rocks and even climb trees

NICHE PARTITIONING

Like coyotes and bobcats, the gray fox hunts squirrels, gophers, field mice, and woodrats. Yet a bobcat can only eat meat, while gray foxes also scarf fruit and even acorns and crickets. Similar species divide resources, so each has a niche. Raccoons, for example, are the most adroit of the midsize carnivores at hunting crayfish in small streams, while the gray fox is very good at going over, under, and around each and every log and stone, foraging with infinite curiosity and a nimble, sure-footed pace.

Counting the tail, these foxes are about three feet long, but the main body is smaller than it looks, and they weigh just ten to twenty pounds. They are smaller and shorter than red foxes (which are all-red with a white-tipped tail), more elongated than a bobcat, and more bushy tailed than feral domestic dogs. Coyotes will cross open fields and highways (albeit at a fast trot), but gray foxes prefer staying in the brushland or following the edge between woodland and meadow.

TEXT ME LATER (OR BETTER YET, JUST PEE ON A BUSH)

Gray foxes mark territory, announce their relationship status, claim dominance, and (inadvertently) reveal what berries are in season through their scat and pee. Except to mate (and while the female raises cubs), they are solitary. Yet they do have ways of sharing news. Foxes have scent glands just inside the anus. Other scent glands are found on their face and the pads of their feet. Our pet dogs do as well, hence their need to scratch the dirt or kick the grass after they have done their business—it is like pasting in your signature line at the end of an email before you hit Send.

Gray foxes are known as "monument markers": you'll often find their scat on top of rocks or logs along trails.

MULE DEER
Odocoileus hemionus

California has only one native deer, the large-eared, long-legged mule deer. It is smaller than the tule elk seen at Pt. Reyes, and not the same as the white-tailed deer of the East Coast, which have different antlers and a white "flag" tail.

* Long legs, tall ears; grayish brown
* If alarmed, raises its small to flash a white butt
* Only males have antlers (shed yearly)

PEST, PAL, OR POT ROAST?

On paper, California's deer population is stable at 450,000, but the California Department of Fish and Wildlife tallies only deer that can be hunted. If we count nonshootable deer (including the ones in Yosemite or in Sonoma backyards), then the state total is more like a million. A hundred years ago, due to hunting and habitat degradation, the deer population in California would have been a small fraction of that. This rebound means we now have as many mule deer as we ever did, going all the way back to pre-European times.

From an ecological perspective, this is good news (though gardeners might disagree). Deer fertilize the soil and keep the plant profile varied, and after the autumn rut, the male's shed antlers provide calcium for rodents. If you like mountain lions, then you have to like deer, which are their primary food.

WHAT IS A DEER?

"Mule" for the ears, which are large and mulish. A deer browses something like eight hundred different plants, including grass, fruit, chaparral, and even lichen. Deer chew cud (like a cow), and only males have antlers, which they shed and regrow each year.

Mule deer can swim well and can cross rivers and lakes. In a fire they will run away, but deer are often seen in the burned area not long after, searching for tender shoots. They also consume ash directly, trying to take in calcium and also potassium, phosphorus, and magnesium. Calcium is delivered by does to their fawns, and it makes up 20 percent of a buck's antlers. This deer-ash-mineral circle is one example of how fire changes the landscape in complicated ways.

Some mule deer in the Sierras migrate to the lowlands in winter, but Sonoma's deer pretty much stay put year-round—or so we think. There is a lot of research yet to be done.

NORTHERN RACCOON
Procyon lotor

This is our familiar bandit-masked, stripe-tailed, hunch-butted night raider of streams, marshes, golf courses, and backyards. The dexterous paws look remarkably like human hands.

- Black mask and black-and-white-striped tail
- Gray-brown body that often looks bunched up or rounded
- Associated with wetlands (but ranges into yards and fields)
- Solitary or in groups; most often seen at dawn, dusk, and nighttime

NUISANCE OR GENIUS?

Raccoons can climb well, and with their nimble paws, they can unlatch trash cans, break into storerooms, or have a go at safecracking the most ingeniously guarded chicken coop. Abroad, they are escaped nuisance species in Europe and Japan, with populations originating from fur farm animals and from escaped pets. And yet, pesky as they can be, don't we admire any modern animal that not merely survives in humanity's shadow but actually flourishes? Sewers, storm drains, roadside culverts . . . where we see just a ditch (or nothing at all), the raccoon sees a good place to fish for crawdads or an underpass to speed up the nightly commute to work.

Because they are mostly nocturnal, raccoons are most commonly seen in a backyard or dashing away in the headlights. Sadly, noting roadkill is one way to determine whether you have raccoons in your neighborhood.

Size varies by age, sex, and access to a back porch full of unguarded dog food, but in general they weigh ten to twenty pounds (up to twice that), and are three feet long, counting the tail. That tail is an important part of the "coonskin cap" of Davy Crockett fame. Raccoon fur was also fashionable for coats in the 1830s in Europe and in America in the 1920s, so if the fad cycles once every hundred years, a third wave of popularity may soon be upon us.

TALL TAIL TALES

All raccoons have striped tails, including this species, a second kind in Mexico, and a third one in Central and South America called the crab-eating raccoon. The usual explanation for the stripes is that if the raccoon is running away, the stripes distract a predator's attention. In a rush, the attacker might lunge at the flashing tail and not at the mud-gray body.

That makes sense, but some of the team working on this book hope the real reason is just that it looks cool.

STRIPED SKUNK
Mephitis mephitis

The iconic skunk is a nighttime rambler whose hind end can produce a powerful jet of noxious nastiness.

- Black and white
- Solitary and nocturnal
- All habitats, including parks and towns
- Beware of the "stink ray" (and keep dogs on a leash)

CONVERGENT EVOLUTION

Skunks are nocturnal, nosing along paths and streams and eating bird eggs, mice, grubs, caterpillars, crickets, fallen fruit, dead fish, and the human rubbish at picnic areas. During the day, they sleep in dens, either self-dug or abandoned by some other animal. They can be active year-round, but in winter rely on fat reserves to help make up for a lack of insects and fruit.

Owls eat them, but land-based predators keep back: a skunk's defensive spray can reach fifteen feet, and it burns the eyes; it also saturates the victim's fur, ruining its ability to wait in ambush undetected. If a dog and skunk have gotten tangled up or a skunk has been hit by a car, the smell lingers on the pavement for a week, especially in rainy weather.

Some animals resonate in our imagination more than others. Even as we have lost track of other nature metaphors, the skunk remains an indelible part of popular culture. Pepé Le Pew is a cartoon skunk on the quest for love. In *The Addams Family*, Uncle Fester wears a coonskin cap made not from a raccoon but from a skunk. If you lose a ball game by a lot of points, you've been skunked, while an ungentlemanly person is nothing but a dirty, lowdown, lying skunk.

SPOTS NOT STRIPES

Our area also hosts a second, smaller, much more elusive species, the spotted skunk. It too is black and white, but the pattern goes in swirls, not a straight line, like a bowl of fudge ripple ice cream. It too has a fluffy, ostrich-plume tail, and it too can send out the stink ray of vomitous death, but this kind is shy, and few people ever see it.

So many nocturnal animals, so little time—and they all remind us of how much we have yet to learn about life after dark.

 Baby skunks, called kittens, are born nearly hairless, but their striped markings are already visible on their skin.

WESTERN GRAY SQUIRREL
Sciurus griseus

This is a large, tree-centric squirrel. By burying seeds and spores, it helps forests continue to be forests.

* Gray and white, and always in or near trees
* Twelve-inch body with a twelve-inch tail
* Active year-round, relying on seed caches in winter
* Forests, oak woodlands, parks, or along streams

JOHNNY APPLESEED SQUIRREL

Everybody likes gray squirrels. Hawks like to eat them, humans like to watch them (but don't feed them peanuts, please), and forests need them to grow. It's true—from pine cones to acorns to buds, squirrels eat what the forest produces. But they also bury some for later. Most they will return to, but some buried seeds survive. From those hidden hoards, new trees begin to grow.

Squirrels also help spread fungi. As we saw on page 17, nature is full of fungi. Some aboveground mushrooms produce spores that get blown by the wind. Other kinds, such as truffles, need rodents—from flying squirrels to tree voles, and especially the western gray squirrel—to process and distribute spores for them. The squirrels seek out underground fungi, and after they digest them, squirrels go poo. Their pellets help the underground fungi find new homes.

Trees are not static sticks, like a kind of leafy telephone pole. They grow and change and talk and share. By spreading fungi, squirrels help maintain the "underground internet."

OTHER LOCAL SQUIRRELS AND CHIPMUNKS

A dun-colored squirrel looks a bit like this one, the California ground squirrel. It lives in burrows, not trees, though some sentinels will perch on a bush or fence post during lookout duty. It is a dirt-lot and open-field animal, not a forest squirrel, and never has an all-white belly.

Two nonnative squirrels occur too. The eastern fox squirrel uses trees and also forages on the ground, so it can look like either a gray squirrel or a ground squirrel. It is gray-brown above and tawny yellow below, never clean white. In our area, it is an urban species seen in parks and neighborhoods. The eastern gray looks like our western gray but is smaller, with a shorter-than-body tail and a tan wash under the gray, as though it was dipped in watercolor paint that didn't quite take.

Easiest to ID is the Sonoma chipmunk. It is our smallest squirrel, found in woodlands and brushy areas, on the ground or in trees. From nose to tail it always has white-and-black racing stripes along its tan body.

CALIFORNIA NEWT
Taricha torosa

A newt looks like a cross between a lizard and a gummy bear. It likes streams and the damp places under rocks or logs. Its orange belly advertises toxic skin—"don't try to eat me."

- Four to eight inches long, including tail
- Pebbly brown skin with orange belly
- Stubby "fingers" and round eyes make it look like a baby (even though it isn't)
- Toxic skin: if you must touch it, be sure to wash your hands right afterward (or better yet, leave it alone and just take a picture)

HOW AMPHIBIANS WORK

Newts are a kind of rough-skinned salamander—all newts are salamanders, but not all salamanders are newts. Both are amphibians and have a two-phase life cycle. The young live in water and have gills. (In frogs, this is the tadpole stage.) The adults of some amphibians absorb oxygen through their skin; some need to stay wet, and others have a secretion that helps keep them moist. That is why we look for newts in the forest's damp, hidden places, where they hunt slugs, worms, snails, and crickets.

Courtship involves dancing and chin-rubbing, a mating ritual called amplexus. Once a male convinces a female that he's the one, he deposits a packet of sperm in the water, which she then takes up into her body to fertilize the eggs. The California newt lays her eggs in a gelatinous mass about the size of a golf ball. As the larvae mature, they wiggle their way out of the golf ball and continue to grow in the water. After spending the first half of their lives in the home pool, by the end of summer or early fall they being to transition into living on land. With the winter rains, they return to the home pools to mate and lay the next season's eggs.

GARTER SNAKE ARMS RACE

The poison on a newt's skin comes from microbes that create a toxin called tetrodotoxin. This is the same poison that puffer fish have and is strong enough to kill anything that wants to eat them—it is many times more lethal than cyanide. Yet one animal is willing to risk it: a garter snake. These snakes seem to be evolving a tolerance of the tetrodotoxin about as quickly as the newts increase the dosage; it could well be that the less well adapted snakes are dying off, leaving only the most resistant ones to carry on. There is a constant "cost-benefit" analysis in play, because becoming increasingly toxic has energy costs for the newt, while becoming increasingly resistant has energy costs for the snake, including an overall decrease in mobility. Each side wants to be just enough "extra" to kill (or eat) the other.

GARTER SNAKE
Thamnophis sirtalis

This common wetland-associated snake comes in many colors and is found in many habitats.

* One to four feet long (two feet is typical)
* Usually striped the "long" way on the body, but highly variable
* Found near water: wet fields, damp forests, or adjacent to streams
* Not harmful to humans (though it will poop on you if you pick it up)

GARTER SNAKES (ARE GOOD FOR YOUR GARDEN)

This slim, attractive snake can turn up in your garden, yet the name is not "garden snake" but *garter* snake, after stripes that look like a strap holding up stockings. Gardeners should be happy to see them, though, since they eat both slugs and mice.

Garter snakes generally hunt in the daytime, not at night, so you are more likely to see this than one of California's other fifty species, some of which are rare and many of which are nocturnal. If you come across a cooperative garter snake and have a need to handle it, they are more likely to poop than bite. Of course, it is very foul smelling poo, and the bite has an anticoagulant that can make your hand throb and swell. As with most things, the choice is yours.

YOUR WARRIOR NAME WILL BE "NEWT BANE"

In the newt entry, we talk about the race between predator and prey. As newts become more poisonous, newt-eating snakes have to become more poison-proof. The garter snake has kept in step and evolved resistance to the newt's deadly toxin. That raises the question, "Why bother? Can't the snakes just go off and eat something else?" The answer is yes and no. Yes, they can eat a variety of things, from tadpoles to bird eggs, but if you can find a menu item that everybody ignores, you can gain a niche behavior that leaves the newts just for you. Even better, the newt's toxins can accumulate inside the snake, making it poisonous as well.

Because the stripes blend into the general flicker of grass and shadows, the garter snake's first defensive choice is to freeze and hope you (or the hunting foxes) stroll past. When the coast is clear, they jet off at remarkable speed. If cornered, they will coil, open their mouths, and look large and fierce. In a tree, they will even flop-hop from branch to branch to escape a predator (or person with a camera).

GOPHER SNAKE
Pituophis catenifer

The gopher snake is a robust snake that looks very "snake-like" and is sometimes mistaken for a rattlesnake. It kills by constriction, though; it does not have venom.

* Two to five feet long (sometimes even bigger)

* Tan with dark blotches or bands; color variable

* Grasslands, woodlands, forest, and farmlands

* If threatened, coils like a rattlesnake and shakes its tail

NATURE'S RODENTICIDE

Gopher snakes will take a bird or lizard or egg, but they specialize in rodents, including wood rats, pocket mice, gophers, voles, ground squirrels, kangaroo rats, and even rabbits. They are constrictors, so they strike, crush, position, and swallow. There have not been many radio-tracked gopher snakes, but home ranges for male snakes seem to be a few acres total.

DON'T TREAD ON ME

Mimicry in nature is common, so that a poisonous butterfly like a monarch is bright orange to warn birds not to eat it, but nonpoisonous ones can be orange as well. The gopher snake is a different kind of mimic, one of action and sound, not bright color. If threatened, it coils, puffs up the body, and cocks the head back ready to strike, while at the same time producing vigorous hissing—matching a rattlesnake so well, even the tail tries to rattle. If danger persists, the gopher snake will fearlessly strike at man or beast. They may not have venom, but their bite is indeed as bad as their bark.

British wartime posters had it right: if you see this snake, keep calm and carry on. Children, horses, and other hikers will all react calmly if you yourself keep cool, and even a large gopher snake is something to celebrate, not fear.

Sometimes a gopher snake will "freeze" in the middle of a trail, hoping you don't see it. Try to resist the urge to pick it up. (If you do, it won't hurt you, but you might hurt it.) Take the opportunity to look closely at its beautiful pattern and deep brown eyes. If you can, note a branch or piece of grass that it has passed, so that you can measure length later, and if you can get a picture to submit to iNaturalist, that's even better.

A sizable gopher snake can prove itself worthy of its name in gopher-disrupted fields. It will check out one mound after another until it finds just the right one, then will punch the entrance open with its nose and plunge into the hole and out of sight. The remaining drama takes place underground, out of sight. After the snake swallows the occupant, it may end up moving into the burrow full-time.

NORTHERN PACIFIC RATTLESNAKE
Crotalus oreganus

This is a venomous snake whose tail ends with a warning rattle. Do use care! They are neither evil nor unevil; they just *are*—an interesting and essential part of nature's great puzzle.

* One to three feet long
* Tan (or gray-green) body with darker brown (or gray or black) diamonds along the back
* Tail ends in stripes and a stacked-button "rattle," often paler than the rest of the snake
* Bite can be fatal: give all rattlesnakes space, and **never** try to pick one up

AGE AND SIZE, MYTH AND REALITY

Flicking rapidly in and out, the snake's forked tongue tastes particles of scent on the air, and can identify not just what an object is but also its size and relative direction. It helps snakes build a 3-D map of their world. They use this not only to track prey but to sort out each other as well. Their version of a dating app is to follow the pheromones, and male snakes have slightly longer, more forked tongues than females, presumably so they can track scents with greater precision.

A female rattlesnake incubates her eggs inside her body, and all rattlesnakes give birth to live young. They possess venom from birth and at first just hunt for small things, such as crickets. As they grow, they can take the adult's preferred food, such as mice and other mammals. They mature at age three and can live ten to twenty-five years.

One of the interesting features about an adult rattlesnake's venom is that it is a hemotoxin—it works through the blood to predigest the prey animal even while it is still alive. So all the snake has to do is hold on long enough for its victim's heart to get the job done.

Contrary to myth, you can't age one by counting the rattles. While it is true that they add a new "button" each time they shed their skin, that shedding can take place once a year or twice a year or even four times a year, and meanwhile, buttons break off over time. Size can be an approximate indication of age, but that too depends on environmental factors.

PLAIN TALK ABOUT RISK

You can die if you are bitten by a rattlesnake and don't get treatment. Do not try to move a live rattlesnake or even pick up a dead one. Don't pose for selfies or take it home in a bag, hoping to cut off the rattles later. *Leave all rattlesnakes alone.*

SIERRAN TREEFROG
Pseudacris sierra

This tiny Gollum frog lives near the ground, but can climb high in trees. Calls often, both in the woods and in Hollywood movies.

* One to two inches long, not counting the hind legs

* Heard more often than seen—*ribbet* (or *krek-ett*)

* Green, gray, or tan with a black mask; can change colors

* Vegetation in and near ponds and ditches; active day or night, year-round

LOUD AND PROUD

The Sierran treefrog is also labeled a tree frog (two words) or as a chorus frog. Our species lives in northern California and the intermountain West, and is closely related to a sister species in the Pacific Northwest and to a third kind in Southern California and Baja.

Treefrogs make a lot of noise, and as usual, you have to blame the boys. From midwinter to midsummer, ponds and streams and marshy areas fill up with sound. You can hear it during the day, but prime time is after dark. To announce that they are ready for sweet lovin', a male treefrog chirrups out a much-too-loud-for-its-little-body *krek-ett* call over and over (and over). These calls both announce their presence and also help them space apart. Since all small frogs look alike in the dark, even to each other, they tell who is who with calls. The sounds can carry a quarter mile. If you check out online recordings, the sound will probably be familiar, either from your own hikes or because it has been picked up by the soundtracks of countless movies and TV shows.

NO CLIMBING GYM NEEDED

Treefrogs climb as well as Spiderman, and probably even better. It comes down to the tips of their very tiny toes. If you look really closely, the rounded toepads turn the ends of the digits into miniature golf balls. A layer of mucous around each toe pad enables them to stick to just about anything, from slick reed stems to a pane of glass. In all habitats, most of their activity occurs at ground level, but if they want to call from high up in a tree, it's an easy ascent.

Frog eggs hatch into tadpoles, which live in ponds and eat plants. As a tadpole turns into an adult, its body absorbs its tail, it grows four legs, and its digestive system switches from a plant-based diet to being ready to be carnivorous.

WESTERN FENCE LIZARD
Sceloporus occidentalis

"Blue bellies" are the "push-up" lizards familiar from gardens, parks, and backyards.

* Four to eight inches long, including the tail
* Backs are tan or gray with dark chevrons; males have blue tummies
* Out in daytime and seen basking on rocks, walls, and logs
* Males do push-ups, particularly in spring and summer

LOOK AT ME! (NO, DON'T!)

Lizards and other small animals have conflicting identities. On the one hand, they don't want to be eaten by a kestrel, so want dull colors and a "scurry in the leaves" lifestyle. (After all, down in the leaf litter is where their food is, the beetles and ants and spiders they hunt.) But on the other hand, they are cold blooded, so sitting in the sun boosts body temperature for free. Further, males want to remind other lizards just how buff and ready to cha-cha-cha they are, and they do that by flashing vivid blue patches. Not too overtly—you don't want something to swoop down and eat you—but just enough so that other dudes at eye level can catch a glimpse of your blue muchness and know not to even bother, you are so eleven on the macho dial.

That is where the push-ups come in: go up on a sun-drenched rock (good for easy warmth) and while there, lift your body high enough to flash a display that is aimed just at the right level, leaving the rest of your body hard to spot by any eyes that might be high up in the predator-filled sky. Other lizard species do this too, but the combination of behavior, color, and habitat make our familiar and abundant western fence lizards easy to spot and easy to identify.

LIKE BUDDHA, THEY HAVE A THIRD EYE

Anybody who's spent time watching lizards notices that they are sometimes light colored and sometimes dark, and usually the darker ones are kind of lethargic. How and why do they change color? Lizards have a "third eye" on the top of the head (actually, it's not an eye, just a special group of cells) that measures the amount of sunlight the lizard is getting. Less sun means darker skin; more sun means lighter skin. Think of it like a solar cell—if the lizard needs more energy, its skin darkens to absorb more light. If it's getting overheated, its skin lightens to reflect the light away.

TICKED OFF

Ticks are tiny, blood-sucking critters that burrow into your skin. More or less everything in nature can get them. Most tick bites are harmless, but in some instances they transmit illnesses, such as Lyme disease (named after a town in Connecticut, not a citrus fruit), which is transferred by a bacterium in the tick's gut. Western fence lizards get ticks too, but in their case, lizard blood has a protein that counteracts the bacterium, so that "post-lizard" ticks no longer spread disease. The ticks have been "cured" or "cleansed."

Thank you, lizards—keep up the good work!

RECOMMENDED HIKES

MENDOCINO

Lakeport

Hopland

Clearlak

LAKE

Gualala

LAKE SONOMA WILDLIFE AREA

Cloverdale

Lake Sonoma

Middletown

Sea Ranch

Black Pt.

Warm Springs Dam

Lake Sonoma ❷

SALT POINT STATE PARK

Russian River

Geyserville

Horseshoe Pt.

Salt Pt.

AUSTIN CREEK STATE REC. AREA

Dry Creek

Healdsburg

Del Rio Woods Regional Park

❸a

ROBERT LOUIS STEVENSON STATE PARK

FORT ROSS STATE HISTORIC PARK

❸b

Healdsburg Veterans Memorial Beach

Calistoga

BOT NAPA STATE NA

Riverfront Regional Park

River

Windsor

❸c

He

Jenner and the Russian River Estuary ❶

Russian River

SONOMA

Mark

West

Spring Lake Regional Park

29

SONOMA COAST STATE PARK

Bodega Bay

Sebastopol

Santa

Santa Rosa

❹

Sugar Ridg State P

❻

Bodega Head

Pacific Ocean

Bodega Bay

TRIONE-ANNADEL STATE PARK

Glen Ellen

Rohnert Park

❺

Jack London State Historic Park

Sono

POINT REYES NATIONAL SEASHORE

Tomales Bay

Petaluma

MARIN

SAN PABLO BAY NATIONAL WILDLIFE REFUGE

Point Reyes

Novato

San Pabl Bay

Lighthouse

Drakes Bay

❶

GOLDEN GATE NATIONAL RECREATION AREA

San Rafael

KEY

❶ Featured Hikes

State and Federal Parklands

N

0 ———— 10
scale in miles

Part 3

EXPLORATIONS AND EXCURSIONS

Kayaks on the beach near Jenner wait for the first paddlers of the day.

FIELD TRIP 1

Jenner and the Russian River Estuary

TRIP AT A GLANCE

* Bald eagles, harbor seals, and winter whales
* Six habitats: river mouth, dunes, marsh, willows, grassland, redwoods
* Family-friendly—toddler beaches to long hikes to beginner kayaking

ESTUARIES: THE "BREAD BASKET" OF THE SEA

The Russian River starts in Mendocino and flows south through Sonoma until it passes through the Alexander Valley in Healdsburg, where it then bends sharply to the west, passing Guerneville and flowing toward the sea. The river enters the Pacific Ocean at Jenner, ten miles south of Fort Ross.

Initially only the Kashaya Pomo lived, worked, ate, and played here. They harvested fish, seaweed, shellfish, and marine mammals, and, inland along Willow Creek, they gathered reeds, sedges, and willow roots for baskets and nets. Redwood bark was used for clothing and basketry. Since 1810, successive occupiers have included the Russians, the Spanish, pre–gold rush fur trappers, and the timber barons of the late nineteenth and early twentieth centuries. They generally arrived in Jenner after having used up the resources someplace else. Today, kayakers and tubers have all but replaced the Russian River's beaver and otters, but beneath the water's surface the salmon and steelhead are

still there, and the river mouth represents a vital example of estuary habitat.

An estuary is a place where fresh water meets salt water and often includes sandbars, lagoons, marshes, and mudflats. It almost always has more species diversity than the adjacent river or ocean. Estuaries matter because they are nurseries for fish and buffer zones to prevent coastal erosion. They are stopovers for migrating birds and stopovers too for bird*watchers*, since the open landscape makes eagles, herons, ducks, and sandpipers easy to spot.

REDWOOD EMPIRE

Jenner was named for a bear-hunting dentist from San Francisco, but for the past 120 years, the main commercial crop has been redwood. To harvest trees, early loggers liked rivers and river mouths, because they could float logs downstream to the mill or build spur-line railroads along the flatter ground. With a good pier and ocean access, the processed lumber could be in San Francisco in two days.

By 1905, the mill at Jenner was producing one hundred thousand shingles a day, plus a variety of planks and beams. Hundreds of workers and their families lived here. The fantasy was that once the trees were clearcut, orchards and vineyards would take their place. But the ecology of topsoil and plant succession doesn't work like that, and soon the redwood empire transformed to sawdust and ghosts.

HUNGRY EAGLES AND PREGNANT SEALS

During the spring and summer, sandbars form at the river mouth. The gray, lumpy things in a pile are all harbor seals, hauled out in order to take a break from watching out for sharks and also to warm up. (They have good blubber, but the water still is cold.) This is a rookery beach, meaning that seals give birth here and raise pups. Among them may be pelicans and cormorants. A cormorant is a snake-necked, duck-size bird that hunts fish by swimming underwater (see page 46). On land, they stand upright like penguins, sometimes spreading their wings to dry in the sun.

Bald eagles hunt fish, if "fish" can include eels and lampreys, and if "hunt" can mean they sometimes snag fish from ospreys rather than catch it themselves. They also will eat rabbits, squirrels, roadkill, and

Harbor seals rest in the sun as a cormorant stretches its wings.

seagulls. Once rare in California due to pesticide poisoning, bald eagles have recovered spectacularly. A pair is usually present at the river mouth year-round, though the all-dark juveniles lack the white head, so may look like large hawks. If you see a juvenile eagle up close, it will be mottled with white streaks and show a black tail band. (The hooked beak is also *massive*.)

You can look for eagles, seals, and (in winter) gray whales from the pullouts on Highway 1 north of Jenner.

EXPLORING ON FOOT AND AFLOAT

A good way to access the estuary is to cross the river on Highway 1 and turn into the Goat Rock Beach parking area at Sonoma Coast State Park. Your goal is to park at the northernmost part of the south side of the river. From the parking lot, two options offer good choices for exploring. If you turn away from the ocean and follow the dune path inland, you go through a stand of Monterey cypress and come out right on the estuary. Toddlers can splash in the shallow water, or you can look for raccoon tracks and study up-close sandpipers.

As you follow the short path across the sand dunes, the low, sage-green plant with the octopus-tentacle flower stalks is beach bur, a native species that colonizes loose sand on ocean-facing dunes. The plant's genus name, *Ambrosia*, is especially accurate if you are the ambrosia plume moth, which feeds on it. You can also reach this side of the estuary by kayaking across from Jenner, directly across on the north bank. The kayak rental outfits there are ready to guide you on an eco-adventure or set you up for your own exploring.

LEFT: Watch for bald eagles perched on snags or sitting right on the beach. **RIGHT:** Just arrived from Alaska, a least sandpiper forages at water's edge. It is the smallest sandpiper in the world.

These young boaters know that nature is fun, not scary.

An alternate way to reach the water is to head north from the parking lot parallel to the coast and to find an overlook at the river mouth where you can see the seals. Don't approach super-close, please—it is illegal, plus they don't need any more harassment.

When hiking or kayaking this part of the estuary, use care in winter. Once the storms open up the lagoon, the river is cold, muddy, and fast, and riptides and heavy surf make the ocean risky too. Spring, summer, and fall visits usually are fine.

SPOTTED OWLS, SALMON, AND THE BACKDOOR TO THE REDWOODS

Big fish start life as little fish, and little fish start in estuaries. An important salmon and steelhead hatchery here is the feeder stream called Willow Creek. The area also protects spotted owls and one of their preferred food animals, the Sonoma tree vole. Voles are like mice, only this mouse lives its life in the tops of trees, eating Douglas-fir needles and drinking condensed fog. The vole's Latin name, *pomo*, honors Native people.

The road to the coast, Highway 116, ends at Highway 1 just where Highway 1 crosses the Russian River. On the south side of the bridge, Willow Creek Road cuts back inland. Drive or bicycle Willow Creek Road to a trailhead for the walk-in Pomo Canyon Environmental Camp. The road is one lane wide at times, and it feels as though you've been inserted directly into the beating heart of the forest. Even if you don't do a hike, drive the road.

An easy hike up Pomo Canyon takes you into redwoods.

Prefer to stay on the coast? Trails go here too.

At the parking area for the campground, follow the dirt road half a mile to the camp, where you can pick up the Pomo Canyon Trail. The redwood forest here, with its cool temperatures and lush understory of sword fern and sorrel, feels very different from the open grassland of the once-logged river valley. You can follow this enchanting trail for 3.5 miles, encountering spectacular vistas of the Russian River and the ocean beyond, and then finish your hike at Shell Beach. (A lot of people like to arrange this as a two-car trip and shuttle back to our starting point.)

Ambitious mountain bikers can continue up the canyon past the campground for a longer workout. The dirt road goes all the way to the Bohemian Highway by the town of Occidental. Early morning riders report seeing bobcats and bears on this trail, so that means you could potentially see a bald eagle, a redwood tree, a gray whale, and a bobcat, all in the same day. Good luck and good hiking (and good riding!).

What will be around the next corner? Maybe a deer or a really good view.

Yellow leaves and low water mean that autumn has come to Lake Sonoma.

FIELD TRIP 2

Lake Sonoma

TRIP AT A GLANCE

* Great place to learn about Native American land stewardship
* Diverse plants; spectacular lake views and mountain vistas
* Loops and side trails offer hikes of one hour to one day

Lake Sonoma is a manmade reservoir created by the Warm Springs Dam, which was completed in 1982. It is managed by the US Army Corps of Engineers. Drought years can lower the lake's size and wet years will raise it, but no matter what the lake is doing, the hiking trails are still there, and with them, an opportunity to think about communities—human communities, plant communities, and the community values expressed by wise land stewardship. The hills around the lake offer spectacular views, and they too offer a chance to think about what the landscape looked like when it was actively managed by First Nation people.

Seen from above, Lake Sonoma looks like a sideways U, with the dam at the east end. Dry Creek Road rises up from Highway 101 at Healdsburg, passes the Visitor Center, then becomes Rockpile Road as it crosses a bridge. You can see a marina and much of the lake from there. Stay on Rockpile Road three miles to No-Name Flat trailhead on the left.

No-Name Flat Trail goes uphill slightly for half a mile before connecting with the Half-a-Canoe loop. When you reach this perch, you will be rewarded with a good view of the lake and surrounding hills. For the full five-mile loop, continue to the right on Half-a-Canoe, or you can do it as an out-and-back of any length. This route takes you through beautiful oak and madrone woodlands, as well as more open grassy areas. The trail's name supposedly comes from the remains of a partial canoe, but if so, the mystery boat is not here anymore.

INDIGENOUS PERSPECTIVES

Our guide is Clint McKay, a member of the Dry Creek Rancheria Band of the Pomo and Wappo Indians. Clint is an educator, basket maker, nature knower, and ethnobotanist. He says that in his tradition, everything starts with the three Rs: "respect, responsibility, reciprocity." Clint speaks modestly yet knowledgeably about how Sonoma's plants can be used and which land-use practices keep them in the best balance. In this section, he shares his insights.

One idea to start with is how anytime we go hiking, we experience a dynamic (not static) landscape. How the landscape is now is not how it was even in the recent past, or how it has to be in the future. There is the trail itself, of course, and that had to be planned, funded, and maintained. But on a larger scale, the history of any given piece of "nature" plays a

Clint McKay emphasizes "respect, responsibility, reciprocity."

Oaks, grasslands, burned pines, and a bathtub ring: the complex realities of Lake Sonoma are all in one view on Half-a-Canoe Trail. As noted in the text, this scene shows both well-stewarded landscape and elements that are no longer in harmony.

role in how that place looks and feels now. There are the natural pro-cesses of erosion and succession, but human processes too.

In Sonoma, that means thinking about such questions as how often fires were encouraged or discouraged from occurring; what kinds of grazing animals have been here previously; how fences partitioned resources; and which nonnative species are present, and who brought them here. Cultural traditions fill landscape with meaning as well—not just origin stories and mythology, but even the simple family history of "This is where my aunt used to come to collect willow shoots to make the foundation for baskets."

This hike can be a good introduction to what we might call "original landscape." For example, it's easy to learn how to spot blue dicks (72) when they are blossoming in the spring. This is a long-stemmed, ground-leafed plant whose flowers can be pink or lavender or blue. Blue dicks can be seen along the trailside in sunny areas; one slope can have

LEFT: Blue dicks can be pink, blue, or purple. The edible bulb is called Indian potato. RIGHT: Wavy-leaved soap plant has many Indigenous uses, from making shampoo to stunning fish.

hundreds. The flowers are small, about the size of a fat pencil eraser, and because the main stems are bare, these plants almost look like grass. Some people know blue dicks as Indian potatoes. That is because underground it has a bulb or "corm," sort of like a green onion. What can you do with it? Clint McKay, who has gathered them all his life, smiles with that look of "What *can't* you do with it?" "It can be eaten raw, fried, roasted, or boiled," he says. This plant sometimes is called blue hyacinth, but that name applies to a variety of flowers, including many that do not grow in California, so we suggest sticking to the usual label. ("Dicks" comes from a Greek word that was part of the original scientific name, though now that named has changed.)

Also common on this trail and other field trips is the wavy-leaved soap plant. It grows a spray of one-to-two-foot green leaves from a central root, which, when dug up, has a fist-size bulb that can be used for many things. If you pulverize that ball and put it in a pool of water, it will stun fish but not kill them. Scoop up what you need, and the others will wake up later, unharmed—a sustainable harvest. This plant can also be used for glue, as shampoo and soap, and as a cleaning brush.

The bay tree or bay laurel (or pepperwood) has long, green, scent-rich leaves (71). These are similar in shape and taste to the Old World bay whose leaves are used in cooking. It is a common tree here, and can be small, midsize, or reach-for-the-sky tall, depending on soil and access to water and the plant's own whims. It flowers November to March, making it beloved by overwintering hummingbirds and also Townsend's and yellow-rumped warblers. Native uses are multiple. "You can cook with the leaves," Clint McKay says, "or treat a cold with the aromatic vapor. Also it has an oil that keeps bugs away in food storage. In winter, collect the 'pepper nuts'—dry them, roast them, grind them, and then make balls like espresso beans."

Two red-barked trees along the trail also have small but edible berries. Manzanitas (80) are typically multitrunked shrubs that are about as tall as a person; the waxy leaves are small and oval. You pick the berries

once they are ripe in summer; after drying them, you can grind that into a very fine powder, "like Pixy Stix," Clint says. The berries also can be boiled into cider.

The Pacific madrone (86) can be one trunk or many, but usually is a proper tree: tall ones aim to be a hundred feet high,

Bay laurel or pepperwood smells good and tastes good, but not to insects. If you're storing things in chests or baskets, this plant wards off pests.

Sunrise lights up a madrone grove.

and even young ones can form a continuous canopy, as in the photo here. Manzanita wood is a darker chestnut and often spirals, with a layer of red, living wood barber-poling beside gray, dead wood. Madrones look more sunburned, with a brighter red color and an outer layer that peels off in papery curls. Both manzanita or madrone have dense, attractive wood. Clint explains, "Madrone wood is good for awls for making baskets. Manzanita wood is good for digging sticks. Both are very useful."

DID JOHN MUIR GET IT WRONG?

How we see the natural world depends how we allow ourselves to see it, and that applies to how we view others. When it comes to Native California, John Muir was one early naturalist who got it really wrong.

The father of national parks and advocate of Yosemite often spoke very ignorantly about American Indians. Trapped between the false dichotomy of the Grand Sublime and "productive" croplands in tidy rows, Muir was blind to other ways of stewarding the land, including low-impact harvesting and the necessity of managing the landscape with fire.

Clint McKay elaborates on this. "John Muir had this philosophy that humans were bad and just needed to leave nature alone. For my people, when we look at the important ghost pine, we see that we need to help steward that tree to stay in balance with the oak woodlands." He explains further, "When you see the Doug firs coming in—trees which were never allowed to encroach before—you see them pushing out other plants and changing the meadows and fields, the open areas where we harvest wild potatoes, wild carrots, wild onions. It is out of balance."

As Clint says, "It's not about us. Humans do not hold dominion over nature. In my tradition, we look at the land for what's in the best interest of *every* living thing in our natural environment. We have to live in harmony with nature, be part of it, keep in balance."

Fire always was a part of this stewardship. The Smokey Bear campaigns have been so successful that now most people assume fire is an "Other" that has to be stopped, prevented, kept out. This is simply not true. Indeed, "for over two million years [people] have used fire," fire ecologist Stephen Pyne reminds us. "They had fire in their shelters, their communities, their fields, pastures, hunting ground, berry-harvesting patches, their paths and song-lines." Fire was a powerful cultural, physical, and psychological force. These people coexisted with fire—"they birthed it, tended it, trained it, related myths about it, and told stories about it."

A good way to see the land the way Clint does is to look at the photograph on page 161. From the trail, we are looking west. We can see the bathtub ring of bare dirt where the lake level has dropped, and, in the foreground, some remnant fences and an open sweep of nonnative grasses. Look closely, though, at the hills across the lake. The lower tier of oak and madrone shows what

LEFT: The size of walnuts, buckeye fruits ripen in summer. BELOW: This spring buckeye is about to ignite in white blossoms.

things looked like historically, before European settlement. Above that is a wide band of burned forest—places where years of fire suppression have encouraged Douglas-fir to fill in too densely. When they burn, it is so hot and closed in, the fire takes everything with it. Clint McKay: "As far as reciprocity and nature, what we put into it is what we get out of it. Even weeds—they may not be useful directly, but could be important for an insect that can pollinate something else. It all connects."

RIGHT: Lake Sonoma offers a chance to see all sizes of wildlife, such as this red-bellied newt. The bright tummy warns predators about the animal's potent toxins.

BELOW: At the base of the dam that forms Lake Sonoma, Warm Springs Hatchery raises coho salmon and steelhead for release into the Russian River.

Del Rio Woods offers good beaches and even better views.

FIELD TRIP 3
The Middle Russian River

TRIP AT A GLANCE

* Three places to get to know the different moods of the Russian River
* All-inclusive access at the middle site, Memorial Beach
* Dogs, kids, bikes, canoes—many recreational styles possible at all three

The Russian River's hundred-mile length includes some popular places to visit, such as Jenner (149) or the wonderful weekend chaos that is Guerneville. This trip—really, three mini-trips in one—encourages us to reclaim nature by exploring other, less-visited river access points. Two of these will be a bit quieter and a bit birdier than traditional sites, while the middle option includes river access for recreationists with disabilities as well as all other adventurers, young and old. All three may require a fee for parking, and of course on busy weekends, all can be crowded or have no parking at all. Learn from the robin: the early bird gets the worm (and the shady parking place).

DEL RIO WOODS REGIONAL PARK

Why does flowing water make us happy? Somehow it just does. At this part of the river, children can wade, dogs can splash after sticks, and dragonflies can dart and hover, wondering why humans are so thick and slow. Unless it is very crowded or very dry, the river here is good for spotting kingfishers and tree swallows (64), while the willows and poppies (70 and 75) blend shimmery greens with bursts of intense orange. In summer, Lake Sonoma releases water in ways that benefit spawning fish downstream, so we may now experience a more stable year-round flow in the Russian River than was true historically. Listen here for singing yellow warblers: *sweet sweet sweet—I'm so sweet!* The songs may be repeated not ten times per day but ten times per *minute*.

To make a good cast, start by wading deep.

BELTED KINGFISHER

One bird you can see at all three sites is the belted kingfisher. It is midsize—like a robin or blackbird—and is slate blue with a long beak and a shaggy mohawk crest. It usually hunts by watching from an overhanging snag (or bridge rail or boat mast)—anyplace where it can see down into the water. A kingfisher also will hover in place to hunt. When it spots a minnow or stickleback, it plunges headfirst into the water, eyes closed, and erupts back out with a squirming prize. It might knock it on a branch before flipping the fish around to swallow it.

Kingfishers also will eat crayfish, mice, frogs, and even shellfish. Hard-to-digest things like spines and fragments of shell are coughed back up in a ball of scales and small bones. They nest in self-dug burrows in the sides of steep banks near water. The nest chamber can be three to six feet deep into the bank; it takes a week or more for the birds to excavate it.

You can often hear kingfishers before seeing them, since both males and females defend their breeding territory, which includes both the embankment and the adjacent upstream and downstream stretches of river. The rattling call carries a long way—you can even hear it inside your car as you pull up to park.

Female belted kingfishers like this one have a chestnut band across the belly. Males are the same slate-and-white combo, but don't have the extra chestnut. Both call with a loud, mechanical rattle.

HEALDSBURG VETERANS MEMORIAL BEACH

True, this park can be crowded on weekends, and true, in low-water years it may not even be open at all, but we want to praise a site that encourages inclusion and access, right in downtown Healdsburg, just downstream from the Memorial Bridge.

Lifeguards watch over swimmers, and free life jackets can be checked out to help less confident swimmers. More important, Veterans Beach offers all-terrain wheelchairs. If you have mobility concerns, these will let you access the river in a new way.

This is also the site of a kayaking concession. Most trips are set up to be one-way: you're shuttled to the start (or picked up at the end), and all you have to do is "go with the flow," gently paddling downstream.

It may not look it, but the steel truss bridge at this beach is historic. It was part of the original Redwood Highway, so was the "101 Freeway" of the day. It was of a popular and universal design: all over America, most towns had a bridge leading into them just like this one. Most now have been replaced, and the bridge here is one of the final thirteen still carrying traffic anywhere in America.

LEFT: An osprey hovers before diving on a fish. Barbed pads on their feet help them grip a slippery catch. **RIGHT:** Riverfront Park includes former gravel pits that have been turned into lakes.

RIVERFRONT REGIONAL PARK

Moving downstream, we come to another of the region's many success stories. What were once gravel pits and waste areas have been combined into a three-hundred-acre park of great beauty. To reach the river, follow the dirt road from the parking area half a mile and then look for side trails on the right. Many people stop before that, though, at the gem-like lakes—equally good for fishing, picnicking, birding, or just getting lost in one's own thoughts.

The dominant trees here are willows, but there are walnuts and redwoods too, and both native California and nonnative Himalayan blackberry bushes. When the authors came here one summer morning, in less than an hour we had seen a gray fox, an osprey, some interesting white flowers we couldn't identify, Anna's hummingbirds, three kinds of woodpeckers, three kinds of swallows, and an underbrush bird with a tan belly and curved, sickle-shaped bill—the California thrasher.

Summer programs include discovery camps and youth kayak lessons. Should we rate this site four out of four stars, or five out of five, or just how many? How about giving it all the stars there are.

This view shows us the "Spring Lake"
part of Spring Lake Park.

FIELD TRIP 4
Spring Lake Regional Park

TRIP AT A GLANCE

* 320 family-friendly acres; horses and dogs allowed
* Next to Howarth Park, Taylor Mountain Regional Park, and Trione-Annadel State Park
* Lake, camping, and swimming lagoon

Come for the Water Bark, the weekend when dogs are allowed in the swimming lagoon, and stay for the ducks and oaks and golden-crowned sparrows. Three "rights" here: right mix of paths and solitude, right price (free except for parking), and right in town, since it's very close to downtown Santa Rosa, just off of Highway 12. Fishing and birding and jogging all are equally possible, and if you're here for a weekend barbecue, be sure to grab a few family members and go look for dragonflies down by the water.

Spring Lake (the lake itself, not the park) is a north-south oval. The Environmental Discovery Center, a parking lot, the swimming lagoon, and the nature trail are on the east (the right side, facing north). A boat ramp and another big parking lot are on the west side, by the parcourse and group campground. Walking paths and a bridle loop connect every possible point in between. To walk around the lake in a circle lets you cover 2.3 miles (or about five thousand steps).

LEFT: Easily seen (and heard), acorn woodpeckers are bold and loud. **RIGHT:** Sparrow-size juncos feed in flocks on the ground, but sing and rest in trees.

BIRDWATCHING FOR BEGINNERS (WITH OR WITHOUT BINOCULARS)

If you've borrowed some binoculars, this is a great place to start to figure out Sonoma's bird species because they are so abundant here, and many are a bit used to people. And even if you don't have binoculars, listening to the morning's warbles and trills is a good way to enter the world of birds now that there are so many apps on your phone to help you identify birdsong. Some apps allow you to record an unknown song, then will help show you what bird it might be.

One bird almost anybody can find. "Loud and proud"—that's how acorn woodpeckers (30) play it. White wing patches flash in flight, so if the yakking call doesn't help you track one down, once it flies from one oak to another (often with an up-and-down rolling, like a rowboat on ocean swells), then the silver dollars on the wings help make it visible. Look for them in the picnic area uphill from the nature center.

Golden-crowned sparrows sing even in winter (48); their plaintive song sounds like "oh poor me." The dark-eyed junco (44) can be found scratching on the lawn alone or with other sparrows or, in spring, singing from a tree by the lake, the way this one is here. Note the dark, hooded head and pale bill on an otherwise plain body. When this one flies away, the white feathers on each side of the tail add visual emphasis—"I'm not just leaving, I am *leaving*."

Mallards and Canada geese nest here, as does a black-and-white flycatcher, the black phoebe. Phoebes sit upright in the lower branches of trees (or perch on playground equipment), tail pumping up and down, plumage looking like a slightly askew tuxedo, waiting for a moth to fly by. When it does, they sally out to snatch it, then usually move on to a new perch a few dozen yards away. Cooper's hawks are interior forest hunters, slim and ambush oriented. While red-tailed hawks circle overhead on the warm afternoon thermals looking for rabbits, Cooper's hawks prefer the morning shadows, sitting imperceptibly still until an unwary sparrow or robin suddenly becomes its breakfast. If a small, long-tailed hawk comes out of nowhere and sends all the little brown jobs scattering in a panic, it means you have just seen this fellow.

Mammals too can be added to your day list, and if you've not yet studied a western gray squirrel (132), they are likely to be in the trees on all sides of the lake. They forage on the ground for acorns and mushrooms, but unlike California ground squirrels (which are also

The western gray squirrel has a bushy tail and a white belly.

here), the gray squirrels will dash up a tree if something startles them. If that "something" was you, the bravest one may sit on a branch, tail waving vigorously, scolding you from just out of reach.

OAKS AND OAK GALLS

By midday, if the birds are napping, let the botany begin. One interesting feature at this park is the oak apples, also called oak galls. If you look up at an oak tree, you often can see many tan apple-like balls growing on branches. These are not fruit but the current or former homes of wasp larvae. The California gall wasp is not even a quarter-inch long, but the growths it causes (the galls) can be as big as a tennis ball.

In fall, the female wasp lays a dozen eggs inside the stem of an oak branch. In spring, the larvae hatch and release a chemical that triggers the gall to form, which will be their home and food source all in one. Young galls look like green apples (please see the four-image grid). In fall, the wasps emerge to lay new eggs. Other insects sometimes join the larvae inside, and woodpeckers may try to open the galls to feed on the tasty bugs inside.

TOP, LEFT & RIGHT: Oak galls are caused by wasps. When fresh, they look like apples; when dried, more like cork tennis balls. **BOTTOM LEFT:** The work of a cluster-gall wasp. **BOTTOM RIGHT:** Spined turban galls on a valley oak.

The dried galls are cork brown and may stay on the tree a few years before falling off. In places without a lot of foot traffic, you may find dozens on the ground.

Other wasps create different kinds of galls. The one shown here that looks like a small red brain is the result of the work of *Andricus confertus*, the convoluted gall wasp. The small brown pyramids on the underside of the leaf in shot four we are pretty sure represent the work of *Heteroecus pacificus*, the beaked spindle gall wasp, but there are two hundred kinds of gall wasp in California, so we admit that we still have a bit more to learn.

If you find a gall on the ground, it is OK to pick it up—it is not dirty, and no wasp will pop out to bite you. The typical large balls seem impossibly light, as if they were made from Styrofoam, not wood. Experts say the galls cost the trees little, and we hope that is true, since most oaks in our area have loads and loads of them.

NINTH STREET ROOKERY, SANTA ROSA

Herons and egrets are colonial nesters, and an aggregate of nests is called a rookery. In spring and summer, there are egrets nesting right in residential Santa Rosa. The rookery is most active from March to midsummer. It is on West Ninth Street between Simpson and Eighth, near Lincoln Elementary.

Look for the adults and young of four species: black-crowned night herons, great egrets, snowy egrets, and cattle egrets. Cattle egrets are originally from Africa (where they follow behind cape buffalo and zebras, which stir up insects in the grass), but in 1877 they ended up in South America, perhaps blown across the Atlantic by a storm. They became established there and spread north, arriving in North America in the 1950s.

Communal nesting offers safety in numbers (with more eyes to watch out for predators), and birds can follow each other to the best feeding grounds. Why nest in a traffic median? A better question might be, Why not? We hope this becomes a trend, and more heron rookeries become established in urban Sonoma.

LEFT: This blue gum eucalyptus is one half of the rookery. A similar tree completes the pair, though latecomer birds are starting to move into some of the adjacent ornamental pines. **RIGHT:** Gawky "tween" egrets can't wait to fledge and move out of Mom's house.

The ruins of Wolf House. The mansion burned down in 1913.

FIELD TRIP 5

Jack London State Historic Park

TRIP AT A GLANCE

* One-mile round-trip hike to famous ruins
* A mix of expected and unexpected plants and birds
* Long-distance trails here as well, plus horseback riding

Jack London remains world famous for adventure stories such as *Call of the Wild*, *White Fang*, and *The Sea Wolf*. He also lectured, traveled the world, and answered some of the ten thousand letters a year that he received. His retreat in Glen Ellen started as a small farmstead and grew to be fourteen hundred acres named Beauty Ranch. He planned a grand estate house here (started in 1911; burned in 1913), and the hike to the ruins makes a popular and easy round-trip hike.

Jack London died in 1916; his second wife, Charmian, did not pass until 1955. In those forty years, she curated the Jack London legacy, doing everything from managing the property to finishing his last books to making sure the estate received royalties from screenplays. The park represents not just his legacy but hers.

Wolf House was the fifteen-thousand-square-foot mansion that burned down just before the Londons could move in. Only stone walls remain today. These are Gothic and fabulous, and look especially gloomy and picturesque on a foggy winter morning. Yet don't stop just with these—the park has another thirty miles of trails besides the pilgrimage route, including trails that are popular with equestrians.

LEFT: Sunburned and slouch-hatted, Jack London rests on the porch after a ride. **RIGHT:** Charmian London, Jack's second wife, managed the estate after his death.

ORDINARY MIRACLES

We like this site because it offers a good chance to learn your "starter set" of nature ID. Most of the oaks are here in this park, including coast live oak, black oak, Oregon oak, canyon live oak, valley oak, and blue oak. And the other "main" Sonoma trees, such as California buckeye and madrone, occur here, and the Sonoma pines, too, including knobcone and gray pine. Incense cedar is a conifer that may trick you into thinking it is a young redwood, since it has cinnamon bark; a tall, straight trunk; and a feathery leaf structure. Coast redwoods usually have browner bark than this tree (it's the High Sierra giant sequoia that has the really red outside bark), and redwoods have small cones with a diamond pattern. Cedars have both large cylindrical cones and buds that are small and split in two like a cartoon duck bill. If there is a broken branch, let your nose decide: cedar wood is used for hope chests and no. 2 pencils, and you will know it when you smell it, especially if you ever chewed on your pencil while taking a test.

To see a particularly interesting redwood tree, take the Ancient Redwood Trail. It leads to the Grandmother Tree, estimated to be 1,800–2,000 years old. Although some coast redwoods grow to be the tallest living things in the world, this particular tree, at fourteen feet in diameter, believes in width, not height. Rather than going for vertical drama, it hunkers down and focuses just on surviving.

Other plants to watch for are ones you may have met before on other hikes, including manzanita and poison oak. Poison oak can be anything from a low bush to a tall, sprawling vine. Just to remind you—since some people get a very strong rash—poison oak always has clusters of inch-long oval leaves that come in threes, and the clusters often include some red or orange leaves, even if it is not yet autumn. (On average, it gets redder in fall and is at its greenest just after winter rains. The leaf structure is always the same, though.)

Birds on your hike may include the oak titmouse, a tiny little guy with a peaked head; both Steller's jays and California scrub-jays; quail; acorn woodpeckers; and a plump gray dove called the band-tailed pigeon. Watch for it up in the tops of pines and oaks; it is the size of a park pigeon, but has a yellow bill and a white band above its dark neck. Males coo deep and low, making a sound like the hoot

Common in woodlands, the titmouse is gray with a tidy mohawk.

of an owl. As these pigeons take off, their wings smack together with a loud clap that helps warn other birds.

EXPECT THE UNEXPECTED

With each visit to the sites in this book, you have a chance to see something that was not there last time. It might be a flower that has bloomed overnight or a new kind of lizard or just the way the sunlight shines on a venerable oak you never noticed before. In winter, look at this park for swarms of ladybugs (called a "convergence"). On one hike, the authors stopped to admire the orange-and-black pattern of an ornate tiger moth, only to realize that it had just laid a single, tiny white egg. We put the egg on a nearby plant—luckily, the tiger moth uses many host plants, not just one species—and left it to complete its business in peace.

Plant ID apps for your phone can help with unusual species like the spice bush pictured here. Checking iNaturalist and eBird before setting out is a good way to preview what others have been seeing and to learn what to watch for yourself. For example, checking the records before a hike revealed that a northern pygmy owl had recently turned up at Jack London, and what a good sighting that was. This diminutive, long-tailed owl comes out in the day (especially in winter) and hunts small birds, which will "mob" it in a communal swarm if they discover it lurking in the neighborhood.

Some days will be only average, true—but that makes them no less miraculous. As Jack London himself has said, "Life is not a matter of holding good cards, but sometimes playing a poor hand well."

TOP LEFT: Poison oak is common in all Sonoma parks. "Leaves of three, leave it be."
TOP RIGHT: An ornate tiger moth rests in a naturalist's hand. **MIDDLE LEFT:** Spice bush has a fabulous red blossom and is endemic to California. **LEFT:** Sticky monkey-flowers bloom from late winter past midsummer.
ABOVE: Male lesser goldfinches have a black cap and a trilling song. They sometimes borrow pieces of other birds' songs.

The vista from Hillside Trail looks past burn scars toward Hood Mountain.

FIELD TRIP 6
Sugarloaf Ridge State Park

TRIP AT A GLANCE

* Short trips or long (we feature an easy meadow-and-forest loop)
* Best chance for deer, fox, bear—the "mega" animals
* Despite successive fires, trails are open and habitat is recovering

Sugarloaf Ridge is a great park, and we could easily have added a dozen bullet points besides these three. For example, "waterfall" didn't make the list, mainly because it depends on rainfall, but it *nearly* did, and besides being a good place to see deer and hawks and squirrels, this park is equally good for butterflies, especially in late spring and early summer. Wildflowers bloom like crazy here most years, and the network of trails invites you to crank out the mileage.

MEADOW TRAIL–HILLSIDE TRAIL–PLANET WALK LOOP

Our recommendation for a first-time ramble is to do the Meadow Trail–Hillside Trail loop, which is two miles out and back, has just a modest gain in elevation (250 feet), and divides the exposure between sun on the outward leg and shade on the return.

To reach the trailhead, leave Highway 12 halfway between Santa Rosa and Glen Ellen, following Sonoma Creek up the narrow but scenic Adobe Canyon Road. Go to the end of the road at the parking area for

Ferguson Observatory. The trail follows the Planet Walk about as far as Saturn before turning back toward the trailhead; to go all the way to Pluto doubles the total mileage.

The idea behind the Planet Walk is that each step represents a million miles of space, and along the way, information signs tell you about the planet you have just reached. It's a fun idea, though as of press time, the signage could use a refresh.

The starting meadow offers flowers, from the familiar California poppy to the tiny white popcorn flower to dense stands of purple vetch. Vetch is native to the Mediterranean and was introduced by Luther Burbank because it helps restore nitrogen in worn-out soil, but it has become naturalized in California, and in spring forms dense stands of pure purple along the trail. Each stem has a vertical row of tubular flowers, each right above the other in a tall stack. The seedpods look like peapods, and the total plant can be anywhere from one to three feet tall. There are lupines here and buttercups; the three-foot-tall plants with a flat-topped bouquet of tiny white flowers are likely to be common yarrow, important for native bees.

With flowers come the flower feeders, such as pipevine swallowtails (116) and smaller ones, such as the hairstreaks. Those are the size of a

A western bluebird watches for insects near the parking lot.

quarter and have blue-silver wings with tiny orange and black dots at the back edge. If you have the patience of a saint (or a macro camera lens, or both), the Russian River watershed hosts about 110 species of butterfly, and that includes groups such as the blues, the coppers, the azures, and the admirals. Don't the names sound attractive? The insects themselves are even better.

Many of our familiar plants from previous trips grow here, including manzanita, coast live oak, soap plant, and both kinds of blackberry—the native and the Himalayan. (Both have edible

Arroyo lupines are California endemics that like chaparral communities and woodlands.

berries, but the Himalayan's are bigger and fatter.)

Yet there is trouble in paradise: on this hike, you can see evidence of a new problem. In the shady parts of the return loop, especially along the creek near the parking area, there are a lot of bay laurel trees and madrone trees. Look at their leaves. Black spots like little squares are signs of a fungus-like infection called Sudden Oak Death, or SOD. This disease is not native to California (it was introduced in the 1990s via nursery plants), and the name says it all. Bay laurel can host the oak death pathogen, but is itself unaffected. The disease also infects rhododendrons and camellias. There is a task force working on what to do next. You can help too. When hiking in muddy conditions where SOD is present, be sure to sanitize your boots when you get home. Spraying your boots with Lysol is one effective way to do this.

NATURE JOURNALING

Keeping a nature journal is always a good idea, and if you want inspiration, one thriving community centers on a website run by John Muir Laws. The Laws site shares online drawing lessons, resources for educators, links to nature journal clubs, and samples of his own extraordinary work. There is no right or wrong way to do journaling, and you don't need to buy anything—you probably already have an old notebook, or you could staple some notebook paper into an ad hoc sketchbook. Drawing or writing helps focus attention and creates a record of sightings and experiences that can be interesting to review later. As the great Harvard scientist Louis Agassiz used to say, "A pencil is one of the best eyes."

Sample page of a nature journal.

Western kingbirds hunt bees, wasps, crickets, and grasshoppers.

GEOLOGY FOREVER

On this hike, you can find serpentine rock, which is green that is speckled with black. It is the California state rock. (We have a state lichen too, something called lace lichen, which is the long, pale-green "witches' hair" seen here on shaded trees.)

Serpentine formed many millions of years ago when lava from the mantel of the earth seeped up between the edges of the tectonic plates. It is not especially dense rock, and with earthquakes and uplift, it has now worked its way upward and arrived at the surface. Most plants don't grow in serpentine soil because it has too much magnesium and nickel and not enough calcium, nitrogen, phosphorus, or potassium.

ABOVE: Most apps can look at a complex scene and still "see" *Sisyrinchium bellum,* western blue-eyed grass. **LEFT:** The phone never lies: there really are bears here! The photo documents a painted lady butterfly investigating fresh bear scat. **OPPOSITE:** A beetle perches on a red flower, which the phone app confirms is *Castilleja foliolosa,* felted paintbrush.

FROM BINOCULARS TO PHONE APPS:
PRO TIPS FOR GOING HIKING

You don't need anything special for going on your first walks. You probably have some sneakers or water sandals that can work, and maybe a hat and sunscreen. If you know somebody who has binoculars, borrow those—and check the lenses on the big and small ends, since they may need cleaning. If you wear glasses, see if the eyecups fold down; to make the binoculars fit the size of your face, look out over a normal scene and bend them in a V until both eyes see the same overlapping circles.

Being out early in the day usually means there will be more animals and fewer people.

Being quiet and wearing drab colors are always better than loud and bright.

Some people are happier with a phone off. Others adore ID apps, and a popular one is Seek by iNaturalist, which can help you identify almost any plant or animal just by holding your phone to it. Can't see that bird in the bush? Use Merlin or BirdNET to identify it by its song.

These apps provide a gateway for beginner naturalists. There are also sky charts and weather apps for the aspiring astronomer—some of these start out free and stay that way; others have fees down the line. Play with the options and see what works for you. The team members behind this book all have used apps on hikes, and we all have left phones off sometimes too.

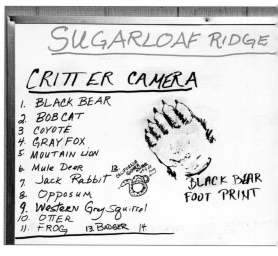

SUGARLOAF RIDGE

CRITTER CAMERA

1. BLACK BEAR
2. BOBCAT
3. COYOTE
4. GRAY FOX
5. MOUNTAIN LION
6. Mule Deer
7. Jack Rabbit
8. OPPOSUM
9. Western Gray Squirrel
10. OTTER
11. FROG

12. CALIFORNIA GOPHER SNAKE

13. BADGER 14.

BLACK BEAR FOOT PRINT

TOP: Come for the poppies, stay for the common woolly sunflowers. **BOTTOM LEFT:** Madrone trees are common along the Hillside Trail. They often look sun-burned. **BOTTOM RIGHT:** A notice board at Sugarloaf Ridge shares recent wildlife sightings.

Serpentine rock also has small quantities of asbestos, so it can't be used anymore as crushed gravel to keep the dust down on dirt roads—another thing not to miss about the old days.

The name "serpentine" comes from the rough texture, which supposedly looks like snake skin. It doesn't, not really, and because this is a good place to see gopher snakes, king snakes, and red racers, we hope you will get the opportunity to compare them for yourself.

The loop ends back at the starting meadow, at the parking lot for the observatory. You have gone to outer space and come back again. *Welcome home*.

Douglas iris and Douglas-fir are named for the same person.

WHERE TO GO NEXT

There are more possible trips in greater Sonoma than there are weekends to do them in, and the team struggled to keep the featured excursions down to a reasonable number. What follows is a list of other parks and preserves to keep in mind, including some that we expect to open in the near future.

LAGUNA DE SANTA ROSA, SANTA ROSA

The Laguna de Santa Rosa watershed forms the largest tributary to the Russian River, draining a 254-square-mile area. Humans have inhabited this area for over eleven thousand years. The Laguna is an important stopover for thousands of migrating birds. Kayaking during a rainy winter is the best way to experience the Laguna's birds, but walking trails are open year-round. lagunafoundation.org

LANDPATHS, SANTA ROSA

A conservation and environmental education nonprofit, LandPaths sponsors guided outings in English and Spanish, community gardens, nature camps and school programs for youth, and volunteer stewardship on its preserves and partner properties.
landpaths.org

MADRONE AUDUBON SOCIETY, SANTA ROSA

This chapter of the National Audubon Society promotes education, enjoyment, and protection of the natural world, especially birds. Field trips are usually free and open to the public. madroneaudubon.org

PEPPERWOOD PRESERVE, SANTA ROSA

Pepperwood manages a thirty-two-hundred-acre biological preserve, an important refuge for more than nine hundred species of native plants and wildlife. The preserve serves as a climate change research venue and a living laboratory for local community engagement via a wide variety of public hikes and classes. pepperwoodpreserve.org

SHOLLENBERGER PARK

A 165-acre wetlands, stewarded by the Petaluma Wetland Alliance. Great birding. petalumawetlands.org

SONOMA COUNTY STATE PARKS

Sonoma's eleven state parks (Armstrong Redwoods, Austin Creek, Fort Ross, Jack London, Kruse Rhododendron, Petaluma Adobe Historic, Salt Point, Sonoma Coast, Sonoma State Historic, Sugarloaf Ridge, and Trione-Annadel) include some of the best scenery and hiking in the country. sonomacounty.ca.gov/services/find-a-state-park

SONOMA COUNTY REGIONAL PARKS

Fifty-four regional parks, trails, and beaches offer something for everyone—abundant spectacular landscapes and recreational and educational opportunities—from the coast to the Russian River to Sonoma Valley. parks.sonomacounty.ca.gov/visit/find-a-park

NEW PARKS IN SONOMA COUNTY

Thanks to voters passing Measure M in 2018, the Sonoma County Agricultural Preservation and Open Space District has been in the process of transferring more than a dozen parcels of land to the appropriate agencies, to provide better access. These will include the California Coastal Trail north of Salt Point State Park; Mark West Creek Regional Park Open Space Preserve; Calabazas Creek, near Glen Ellen; the Wright Hill and Carrington Ranch properties on the Sonoma coast; and Dutch Bill Creek property in Monte Rio. Future park expansions are planned for Crane Creek, Helen Putnam, Hood Mountain, North Sonoma Mountain, and Sonoma Valley Regional Parks.

LEFT: Damp forest + recent rain = best time to hunt for mushrooms. **BELOW:** Well-named barn swallows do indeed nest in old barns. **BOTTOM:** A bobcat hears the shutter's click and looks up.

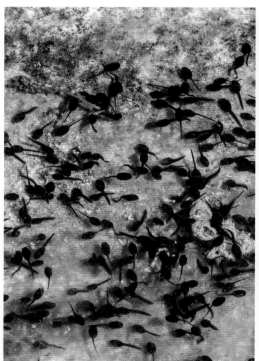

TOP: A turkey vulture rides an air current, its wings held in a shallow V. LEFT: Tadpoles gorge on algae in a sun-warmed pond. RIGHT: A Cooper's hawk waits on a wall, alert for juncos and sparrows.

ABOUT THE AUTHORS

Poet, naturalist, and photographer **CHARLES HOOD** is the author of the Heyday collection *A Salad Only the Devil Would Eat: The Joys of Ugly Nature*. His other Heyday titles include field guides to mammals and birds, and for the Natural History Museum of Los Angeles County he was the lead author and photographer for *Wild LA*, which the California Independent Booksellers Alliance named a Best Nonfiction Book for 2019. Charles stopped counting birds when he reached five thousand species, but says that his replacement addiction is to keep a world mammal list.

LYNN HOROWITZ is an avid hiker, certified California Naturalist, and longtime Sonoma County resident. She served as an interpretive docent at Tilden Park and UC Botanical Garden and founded an ESL school for vineyard workers' families. For the past thirty years, she and her husband, Jeff, have owned and operated a two-hundred-acre ranch and vineyard in the Alexander Valley, where she first conceived of a guide to the wine country's natural beauty and landscapes.

JOHN MUIR LAWS is a naturalist, educator, writer, and artist, with degrees in conservation and resource studies from the University of California, Berkeley; in wildlife biology from the University of Montana, Missoula; and in scientific illustration from the University of California, Santa Cruz. He is the author of *The Laws Guide to Nature Drawing and Journaling, The Laws Guide to the Sierra Nevada*, and *How to Teach Nature Journaling*, among others. Visit his website at johnmuirlaws.com.

JEANNE WIRKA is an ecologist and nature writer with over twenty-five years of experience in conservation science, ecological restoration, and environmental education. As the resident biologist at Sonoma County's Bouverie Preserve from 2005 to 2018, she taught field courses in plant ecology, wildflower identification, mammals, birds, reptiles, amphibians, insects, fungi, fire ecology, and ecological principles. She is currently the resident ecologist at the Center for Land-Based Learning in Woodland, California.

PHOTO PERMISSIONS